Cambridge Latin Course

SECOND EDITION

Unit I

One volume edition

CAMBRIDGE UNIVERSITY PRESS

Cambridge
London New York New Rochelle
Melbourne Sydney

for the SCHOOLS COUNCIL

Published by the Press Syndicate of the University of Cambridge
The Pitt Building, Trumpington Street, Cambridge CB2 1RP
32 East 57th Street, New York, NY 10022, USA
296 Beaconsfield Parade, Middle Park, Melbourne 3206, Australia.

© Schools Council Publications 1970, 1982

First published 1970
Reprinted 1971, 1972, 1973, 1974, 1975, 1978, 1979, 1980
Second edition 1982

Printed in Great Britain at the University Press, Cambridge

Library of Congress catalogue card number: 82-4240

ISBN 0 521 28740 5

Contents

Caecilius

Caecilius est pater.

Metella est māter.

Quīntus est fīlius.

Clēmēns est servus.

Grumiō est coquus.

Cerberus est canis.

Caecilius est in tablīnō.

Metella est in ātriō.

Quīntus est in triclīniō.

Clēmēns est in hortō.

Grumiō est in culīnā.

Cerberus est in viā.

pater est in tablīnō.
pater in tablīnō scrībit.

māter est in ātriō.
· māter in ātriō sedet.

fīlius est in triclīniō.
fīlius in triclīniō bibit.

servus est in hortō.
servus in hortō labōrat.

coquus est in culīnā.
coquus in culīnā labōrat.

canis est in viā.
canis in viā dormit.

Words and phrases

est	is	in triclīniō	in the dining-room
pater	father	in hortō	in the garden
māter	mother	in culīnā	in the kitchen
fīlius	son	in viā	in the street
servus	slave	scrībit	is writing
coquus	cook	sedet	is sitting
canis	dog	bibit	is drinking
in tablīnō	in the study	labōrat	is working
in ātriō	in the hall	dormit	is sleeping

Cerberus

Caecilius est in hortō. Caecilius in hortō sedet. servus est in ātriō. servus in ātriō labōrat. Metella est in ātriō. Metella in ātriō sedet. Quīntus est in tablīnō. Quīntus in tablīnō scrībit. Cerberus est in viā.

coquus est in culīnā. coquus in culīnā dormit. Cerberus intrat. 5
Cerberus circumspectat. cibus est in mēnsā. canis salit. canis in mēnsā stat. Grumiō stertit. canis lātrat. Grumiō surgit. coquus est īrātus. 'pestis ! furcifer !' coquus clāmat. Cerberus exit.

Words and phrases

intrat	enters	lātrat	barks
circumspectat	looks round	surgit	gets up
cibus	food	īrātus	angry
in mēnsā	on the table	pestis !	pest !
salit	jumps	furcifer !	scoundrel !
stat	stands	clāmat	shouts
stertit	snores	exit	goes out

About the language

1 Latin sentences containing the word 'est' often follow an order similar to that of English.

for example:

Metella est māter.   canis est in viā.
Metella is the mother.   The dog is in the street.

2 In other Latin sentences, the order is usually different from that of English.

for example: canis in viā dormit.
                         The dog is sleeping in the street.

                         servus in culīnā labōrat.
                         The slave is working in the kitchen.

Practising the language

1 Complete each sentence with a suitable word from the list below. Write out the completed sentence in Latin and then translate it into English.

Quīntus, Grumiō, Caecilius, canis, māter, servus

for example: . . . . . . est in hortō.
                         servus est in hortō.
                         The slave is in the garden.

1 . . . . . . est in hortō.   4 . . . . . . est in tablīnō.
2 . . . . . . est in viā.   5 . . . . . . est in ātriō.
3 . . . . . est in culīnā.   6 . . . . . . est in triclīniō.

2 Complete each sentence with a suitable phrase from the list below. Write out the completed sentence in Latin and then translate it into English.

in viā, in hortō, in ātriō, in tablīnō, in culīnā, in triclīniō

1 Clēmēns . . . . . . labōrat.   4 Metella . . . . . . stat.
2 Caecilius . . . . . . scrībit.   5 coquus est . . . .
3 canis . . . . . . lātrat.   6 Quīntus est . . . .

Caecilius

Caecilius lived in Italy during the first century A.D. in the town of Pompeii. This town had a population of about 20,000, and was situated at the foot of Mount Vesuvius on the coast of the Bay of Naples. Caecilius was a rich Pompeian banker. His business accounts, which were discovered when his house was dug up, tell us that he was also an auctioneer, tax-collector, farmer and money-lender.

He inherited some of his money from his father, Lucius Caecilius Felix, but he probably obtained most of it through his own shrewd and energetic business activities. He dealt in slaves, cloth, timber and property. He also carried on a cleaning and dyeing business, grazed herds of sheep or cattle on pastureland outside the town, and he sometimes won the contract for collecting the local taxes. He may have owned a few shops as well, and probably lent money to local shipping companies wishing to trade with countries overseas. The profit on such trade was often very large.

We can discover more about Caecilius by studying his full name, which was Lucius Caecilius Iucundus. Only a Roman citizen would have three names. A slave would have only one, such as Clemens or Grumio. As a Roman citizen, Caecilius not only had the right to vote in elections, but also was fully protected by the law against unjust treatment. The slaves who lived and worked in his house and in his businesses had no rights of their own. They were his property and he could treat them well or badly as he wished. There was one important exception to this rule. The law did not allow a master to put a slave to death without showing good reason.

Caecilius' first name was Lucius. This was the personal name of Caecilius himself, rather like a modern first name. His second name was Caecilius and this shows that he was a member of the 'clan' of the Caecilii. Clans or family groups were very important, and strong feelings of loyalty existed within them. Caecilius' third name, Iucundus, is the name of his own family and close relatives. The word 'iūcundus' means 'pleasant', just as in English we find surnames like Merry or Jolly. Whether Caecilius was in fact a pleasant character, you will find out from the stories that you read about him.

Houses in Pompeii

The house in which a wealthy man like Caecilius lived differed in several ways from a modern house. The house came right up to the pavement; there was no garden or grass in front of it. The windows were few, small and placed fairly high up. They were intended to let in enough light, but to keep out the heat of the sun. Large windows would have made the rooms uncomfortably hot in summer and cold in winter.

The houses usually stood only one storey high. Some houses in Pompeii, however, had a second storey above. From the outside, with its few windows and high walls stretching all the way round, the house did not look very attractive or inviting. It was deliberately designed to shut out noise and heat and to provide as much privacy as possible.

The ground plan of the house shows two parts or areas of about equal size. They look like courtyards surrounded by rooms opening off the central space. Let us look at these two parts more closely.

Plan of a Pompeian house

1 impluvium	pool for rain-water
2 triclīnium	dining-room
3 tablīnum	study
4 larārium	shrine of the household gods
5 cubiculum	bedroom
6 summer triclīnium	
7 culīna	kitchen
8 latrīna	lavatory

The main entrance to the house was in the side facing the street. It consisted of a tall double door. The Latin word for this door was 'iānua'. On passing through the door, the visitor came into a short corridor which led straight into the main hall or 'ātrium'. This was the most important part of the house. It was large and high and contained little furniture. The roof sloped down slightly towards a large square opening in the middle. The light streamed in through the opening, high overhead. Immediately below was a shallow rectangular pool, lined with marble, which received the rain-water. Round the atrium were arranged the main rooms used by the master's family, the bedrooms, study and dining-room. The entrances to these rooms were not usually provided with a wooden door, but with a heavy curtain that could be drawn across.

One of the most striking things about the atrium was the sense of space. The high roof with the glimpse of sky through the central opening, the large floor area and the absence of much furnishing all helped to give this impression. The only furniture to be seen was a bronze or marble table, a couch, and a chest in which the family treasures were stored. In a corner, near the main door, there was a small shrine at which the family gods were worshipped. The floor was paved with plain marble slabs.

The walls of the atrium were decorated with panels of brightly painted plaster. The Pompeians were especially fond of red, orange and blue. On many of these panels there were paintings of scenes from well-known stories, especially the myths of the Greeks.

Three-legged table in the tablinum of the House of Paquius Proculus

From this first area of the house, the visitor passed by way of the 'tablīnum' (study) or through a passage into the second part. This was the 'peristȳlium'. It was a garden surrounded by a colonnade of pillars. Around the colonnade were the kitchen, the lavatory, the summer dining-room, slaves' quarters and storage rooms. Some houses also had their own set of baths. Like the atrium, the colonnade was often elaborately decorated. In the centre of this area was an ornamental garden, where flowers and shrubs were laid out in a careful plan. In the small fish-pond in the middle, a fountain threw up a jet of water, and marble statues of gods and heroes stood here and there. In the peristylium, the members of the family enjoyed sunshine or shade as they wished; here they relaxed on their own or entertained a few close friends.

Only well-to-do families could afford houses like this; most people lived in much simpler homes. Some of the poorer shopkeepers had only a few rooms above their shops. In large cities such as Rome, many people lived in blocks of flats several storeys high.

Words and phrases checklist

You have now met the following words three times or more. Check that you are able to translate them.

ātrium	hall
canis	dog
coquus	cook
est	is
fīlius	son
hortus	garden
in	in
labōrat	works, is working
māter	mother
pater	father
sedet	sits, is sitting
servus	slave
via	street

in vīllā

amīcus

Caecilius est in ātriō.

amīcus Caecilium salūtat.

Metella est in ātriō.

amīcus Metellam salūtat.

Quīntus est in ātriō.

amīcus Quīntum salūtat.

servus est in ātriō.

amīcus servum salūtat.

canis est in ātriō.

amīcus canem salūtat.

Metella

coquus est in culīnā.

Metella culīnam intrat.

Grumiō labōrat.

Metella Grumiōnem spectat.

cibus est parātus.

Metella cibum gustat.

Grumiō est anxius.

Metella Grumiōnem laudat.

amīcus est in hortō.

Metella amīcum vocat.

mercātor

amīcus Caecilium vīsitat. amīcus est mercātor. mercātor vīllam intrat. Clēmēns est in ātriō. Clēmēns mercātōrem salūtat. Caecilius est in tablīnō. Caecilius pecūniam numerat. Caecilius est argentārius. amīcus tablīnum intrat. Caecilius surgit.

'salvē !' Caecilius mercātōrem salūtat.   5

'salvē !' mercātor respondet.

Caecilius triclīnium intrat. amīcus quoque intrat. amīcus in lectō recumbit. argentārius in lectō recumbit.

Grumiō in culīnā cantat. Grumiō pāvōnem coquit. coquus est laetus. Caecilius coquum audit. Caecilius nōn est laetus. Caecilius   10 cēnam exspectat. amīcus cēnam exspectat. Caecilius Grumiōnem vituperat.

Words and phrases

mercātor	merchant
amīcus	friend
vīsitat	is visiting
vīllam	house
salūtat	greets

pecūniam
  numerat
	is counting
	  money

argentārius	banker
salvē !	hello !
respondet	replies
quoque	also

in lectō
  recumbit
	reclines
	  on a couch

cantat	is singing
pāvōnem	peacock
coquit	is cooking
laetus	happy
audit	hears
nōn est	is not
cēnam	dinner
exspectat	is waiting for
vituperat	blames, curses

in triclīniō

Grumiō triclīnium intrat. Grumiō pāvōnem portat. Clēmēns triclīnium intrat. Clēmēns vīnum portat. Caecilius pāvōnem gustat.

   'pāvō est optimus !' Caecilius clāmat.

   mercātor quoque pāvōnem gustat. mercātor cēnam laudat. dominus coquum laudat. Grumiō exit.   5

   ancilla intrat. ancilla suāviter cantat. ancilla dominum dē-lectat. ancilla mercātōrem dēlectat. mox dominus dormit. amīcus quoque dormit.

   Grumiō triclīnium intrat et circumspectat. coquus cibum in mēnsā videt. Grumiō cibum cōnsūmit et vīnum bibit ! Caecilius   10 Grumiōnem nōn videt. coquus in triclīniō magnificē cēnat.

   coquus ancillam spectat. ancilla Grumiōnem dēlectat. Grumiō ancillam dēlectat. Grumiō est laetissimus.

Words and phrases

portat	is carrying
vīnum	wine
gustat	tastes
optimus	very good, excellent
laudat	praises
dominus	master
ancilla	maid, slave-girl
suāviter	sweetly
dēlectat	pleases
mox	soon
et	and
videt	sees
cibum cōnsūmit	eats the food
magnificē	magnificently, in style
cēnat	dines, has dinner
spectat	looks at
laetissimus	very happy

About the language

1 You have now met two forms of the same word:

Caecilius - Caecilium   Metella - Metellam
mercātor - mercātōrem

2 The different forms are known as the *nominative case* and the *accusative case*.

nominative	accusative
Caecilius	Caecilium
Metella	Metellam
mercātor	mercātōrem

3 If Caecilius performs an action, such as praising Grumio, the nominative 'Caecilius' is used:

Caecilius Grumiōnem laudat.
Caecilius praises Grumio.

4 But if somebody else does something to Caecilius, the accusative 'Caecilium' is used:

amīcus Caecilium salūtat.
The friend greets Caecilius.

5 Notice the difference in word order between Latin and English:

coquus culīnam intrat.
The cook enters the kitchen.

Clēmēns vīnum portat.
Clemens carries the wine.

Practising the language

1 Complete each sentence with a suitable word or phrase from the list below. Write out the completed sentence in Latin and then translate it into English.

scrībit, in culīnā, servus, amīcus, sedet, in viā

for example: canis . . . . . . stat.
canis in viā stat.
The dog is standing in the street.

1 Grumiō . . . . . . coquit.
2 . . . . . . in hortō labōrat.
3 mercātor in tablīnō . . . . . .
4 Cerberus . . . . . . dormit.
5 Metella in ātriō . . . . . .
6 . . . . . . in triclīniō cēnat.

2 Complete each sentence with a word that makes good sense, choosing your answer from the words in brackets. Write out the completed sentence in Latin and then translate it into English.

for example: amīcus Caecilium . . . . . . (sedet, vīsitat)
amīcus Caecilium vīsitat.
A friend visits Caecilius.

1 Caecilius pecūniam . . . . (numerat, dormit)
2 Clēmēns vīnum . . . . . . (labōrat, portat)
3 ancilla hortum . . . . . . (intrat, gustat)
4 Metella mercātōrem . . . . (salūtat, cantat)
5 Quīntus cibum . . . . . . (vīsitat, cōnsūmit)
6 servus vīllam . . . . . . (dormit, intrat, portat)
7 amīcus Grumiōnem . . . . (spectat, stat, recumbit)
8 māter fīlium . . . . . . (surgit, dormit, vituperat)
9 mercātor canem . . . . . . (sedet, cōnsūmit, audit)
10 dominus ancillam . . . . . . (scrībit, laudat, numerat)

3   Translate into English:

amīcus Grumiōnem vīsitat. amīcus est servus. servus vīllam
intrat. Clēmēns est in ātriō. servus Clēmentem videt. Clēmēns
servum salūtat. servus culīnam intrat. servus culīnam circumspectat.

Grumiō nōn est in culīnā. servus cibum videt. cibus   5
est parātus ! servus cibum gustat. cibus est optimus.

Grumiō culīnam intrat. Grumiō amīcum videt. amīcus
cibum cōnsūmit ! coquus est īrātus.

'pestis! furcifer!' coquus clāmat. coquus amīcum vituperat.

parātus   ready

Food excavated at Pompeii: (top) walnuts, (bottom) a loaf, (right) grain

Daily life

The day began early for Caecilius and the members of his household. He would usually get up at dawn. His slaves were up even earlier, sweeping and dusting and polishing. Caecilius did not spend much time dressing. The first garment that he put on was his tunic, similar to a short-sleeved shirt, then his toga, which was a large woollen cloak arranged in complicated folds, and finally his shoes, which were rather like modern sandals. A quick wash of the hands and face with cold water was enough at that time of the morning; later he would visit a barber and be shaved; and in the afternoon he would take a long leisurely bath.

His wife, Metella, also got up early. She was responsible for the smooth running of the household, and had to organise and supervise the work of the domestic slaves. She would also prepare carefully for social occasions, such as the entertainment of guests. With the help of a skilled slave-woman, she did her hair in the latest style, put on her make-up, including powder, rouge and mascara, and arranged her jewellery, of which she had a large and varied collection.

Breakfast was only a light snack. It was often no more than a cup of water and a piece of bread. The first duty of the day for Caecilius was to receive the respectful greetings of a number of poorer people and freedmen who had previously been his slaves. To these visitors he distributed small sums of money, and, if they were in any kind of trouble, he gave them as much help and protection as he could. In return they helped Caecilius in several ways; for example, they accompanied him as a group of supporters on public occasions, and they might also be employed by him in business affairs. They were known as his 'clientēs' and he was their 'patrōnus'. When Caecilius had finished seeing his clientes, he set out for the 'forum', or market-place, where he spent the rest of the morning trading and banking.

Lunch was eaten about midday and this also was a light meal. It usually consisted of some meat or fish followed by fruit. Business

A dining-room

The arrows show
the position of
the people dining.

ended soon after lunch. Caecilius would then have a short
siesta before going to the baths. Towards the end of the afternoon,
the main meal of the day began. This was called 'cēna'.

During the winter Caecilius used the inner dining-room near the
atrium; but in the summer he would generally have preferred the
dining-room at the back of the house which looked straight out onto
the garden. Three couches were arranged round a circular table.
This dining-table, though small, was very elegantly carved and
decorated. Each couch had places for three people. The diners
reclined on these couches, leaning on their left elbow and taking
food from the table with their right hand. The food was cut up by a
slave before being served and the diners ate it with their fingers or a
spoon. Forks were not used by the Romans. Not all Romans
reclined when eating dinner, but it was usual among rich or
upper-class families; poor people, slaves and children would eat
sitting up.

The meal began with a first course of light dishes to whet the appetite. Eggs and fish were often served. Then came the main course, in which a variety of meat dishes would be offered. Beef, pork, mutton and poultry were all popular and in preparing them the cook would do his best to show off his skill and imagination. Finally, the dessert was brought in, consisting of fruit and cheese. Wine produced locally from the vineyards on Vesuvius was drunk throughout the meal. There was no hurry, for this was the big social occasion of the day. With much talk and laughter, with music and singing, the exchange of gossip and drinking of toasts, dinner sometimes went on until late in the evening.

Words and phrases checklist

You have now met the following words three times or more. Check that you are able to translate them.

amīcus	friend
ancilla	slave-girl, maid
cēna	dinner
cibus	food
dominus	master
dormit	sleeps
gustat	tastes
intrat	enters
laetus	happy
laudat	praises
mēnsa	table
mercātor	merchant
quoque	also
salūtat	greets

Pantagathus, Celer, Syphāx

in forō

Caecilius nōn est in vīllā. Caecilius in forō labōrat. Caecilius est
argentārius. argentārius pecūniam numerat.

Caecilius forum circumspectat. ecce ! pictor in forō ambulat.
pictor est Celer. Celer Caecilium salūtat.

ecce! tōnsor quoque est in forō. tōnsor est Pantagathus. Caecilius   5
tōnsōrem videt.

'salvē !' Caecilius tōnsōrem salūtat.

'salvē !' Pantagathus respondet.

ecce ! vēnālīcius forum intrat. vēnālīcius est Syphāx. vēnālīcius
mercātōrem exspectat. mercātor nōn venit. Syphāx est īrātus.   10
Syphāx mercātōrem vituperat.

Words and phrases

in forō	in the forum
ecce !	see ! look !
pictor	painter, artist
ambulat	is walking
tōnsor	barber
vēnālīcius	slave-dealer
nōn venit	does not come

pictor

pictor ad vīllam venit. pictor est Celer. Celer iānuam pulsat.
Clēmēns pictōrem nōn audit. servus est in hortō. Celer clāmat.
canis Celerem audit et lātrat. Quīntus canem audit. Quīntus ad
iānuam venit. fīlius iānuam aperit. Celer Quīntum salūtat et vīllam
intrat.   5

　　Metella est in culīnā. Quīntus mātrem vocat. Metella ātrium
intrat. pictor Metellam salūtat. Metella pictōrem ad triclīnium
dūcit.

　　Celer in triclīniō labōrat. Celer pictūram pingit. magnus leō est in
pictūrā. Herculēs quoque est in pictūrā. leō Herculem ferōciter   10
petit. Herculēs magnum fūstem tenet et leōnem verberat. Herculēs
est fortis.

　　Caecilius ad vīllam revenit et triclīnium intrat. Caecilius
pictūram intentē spectat et pictūram laudat.

Words and phrases

ad vīllam	to the house
iānuam pulsat	knocks at the door
ad iānuám	to the door
aperit	opens
vocat	calls
dūcit	leads
pictūram pingit	paints a picture
magnus	big
leō	lion
ferōciter	fiercely
petit	makes for, attacks
fūstem	club
tenet	is holding
verberat	is striking
fortis	brave
revenit	returns
intentē	intently

When you have read this story, answer the questions at the end.

tōnsor

tōnsor in tabernā labōrat. tōnsor est Pantagathus. Caecilius intrat.
   'salvē, tōnsor !' inquit Caecilius.
   'salvē !' respondet Pantagathus.
   tōnsor est occupātus. senex in sellā sedet. Pantagathus
novāculam tenet et barbam tondet. senex novāculam intentē   5
spectat.
   poēta tabernam intrat. poēta in tabernā stat et versum recitat.
Caecilius rīdet, sed tōnsor nōn rīdet. versus est scurrīlis; tōnsor est
īrātus.
   'furcifer ! furcifer !' clāmat Pantagathus. senex est perterritus.   10
tōnsor barbam nōn tondet. tōnsor senem secat. multus sanguis fluit.
   Caecilius surgit et ē tabernā exit.

Barber's shears

Words and phrases

in tabernā	in the shop	versum recitat	recites a line, recites a verse
inquit	says		
occupātus	busy	rīdet	laughs, smiles
senex	old man	sed	but
in sellā	in the chair	scurrīlis	rude
novāculam	razor	perterritus	terrified
barbam tondet	is trimming his beard	secat	cuts
		multus	much
poēta	poet	sanguis fluit	blood flows
		ē tabernā	out of the shop

Questions

1   Who is working in the shop when Caecilius arrives ? What is he doing ?
2   Who comes into the shop after Caecilius ? What does he do ?
3   Why is the barber angry ?
4   What happens to the old man ?
5   What does Caecilius do ? Why ?

vēnālīcius

Caecilius ad portum ambulat. Caecilius portum circumspectat.
argentārius nāvem Syriam videt, et ad nāvem ambulat. Syphāx
prope nāvem stat.

'salvē, Syphāx !' clāmat argentārius. Syphāx est vēnālīcius.
Syphāx Caecilium salūtat.   5

Caecilius servum quaerit. Syphāx rīdet. ecce ! Syphāx magnum
servum habet. Caecilius servum spectat. argentārius nōn est
contentus. argentārius servum nōn emit.

'vīnum !' clāmat Syphāx. ancilla vīnum ad Caecilium portat.
argentārius vīnum bibit.   10

Caecilius ancillam spectat. ancilla est pulchra. ancilla rīdet.
ancilla Caecilium dēlectat. vēnālīcius quoque rīdet.

'Melissa cēnam optimam coquit', inquit vēnālīcius. 'Melissa
linguam Latīnam discit. Melissa est docta et pulchra. Melissa . . .'

'satis ! satis !' clāmat Caecilius. Caecilius Melissam emit et ad   15
vīllam revenit. Melissa Grumiōnem dēlectat. Melissa Quīntum
dēlectat. ēheu ! ancilla Metellam nōn dēlectat.

Words and phrases

ad portum	to the harbour	pulchra	beautiful
nāvem Syriam	Syrian ship	linguam Latīnam	Latin language
prope nāvem	near the ship	discit	is learning
quaerit	is searching for, is looking for	docta	skilful, good at her job
habet	has	satis	enough
contentus	satisfied	ēheu !	alas !
emit	buys		

About the language

1 Notice the difference between the nominative case and the accusative case of the following words:

nominative	Metella	Caecilius	mercātor
accusative	Metellam	Caecilium	mercātōrem

2 A large number of words, such as 'ancilla' and 'taberna', form their accusative in the same way as 'Metella'. They are known as the *first declension*, and look like this:

nominative	Metella	ancilla	taberna
accusative	Metellam	ancillam	tabernam

3 Another large group of words is known as the *second declension*. Most of these words form their accusative in the same way as 'Caecilius'.
For example:

nominative	Caecilius	servus	amīcus
accusative	Caecilium	servum	amīcum

4 You have also met several words belonging to the *third declension*.
For example:

nominative	mercātor	leō	senex
accusative	mercātōrem	leōnem	senem

The nominative of the third declension may take various forms; but the accusative nearly always ends in '-em'.

Practising the language

1 Complete each sentence with a word that makes good sense, choosing your answer from the words in brackets. Write out the completed sentence in Latin and then translate it into English.

1 mercātor ē vīllā . . . . . . (quaerit, ambulat)
2 servus ad hortum. . . . . . (recitat, venit)
3 coquus ad culīnam . . . . . . (revenit, habet)
4 Syphāx servum ad vīllam . . . . . . (dūcit, ambulat)
5 Clēmēns cibum ad Caecilium . . . . . . (salit, venit, portat)

2 Complete each sentence with the right word, choosing your answer from the words in brackets. Write out the completed sentence in Latin and then translate it into English.

for example: . . . . . . vīnum portat. (servus, servum)
                servus vīnum portat.
                The slave carries the wine.

1 amīcus . . . . . . laudat. (servus, servum)
2 senex . . . . . . intrat. (taberna, tabernam)
3 . . . . . . cibum gustat. (dominus, dominum)
4 . . . . . . Metellam salūtat. (mercātor, mercātōrem)
5 vēnālīcius . . . . . . videt. (tōnsor, tōnsōrem)
6 . . . . . . versum recitat. (poēta, poētam)
7 . . . . . . in forō ambulat. (senex, senem)
8 ancilla . . . . . . ad ātrium dūcit. (pictor, pictōrem)

The town of Pompeii

The town of Pompeii was built on a low hill of volcanic rock about eight kilometres (five miles) south of Mount Vesuvius and close to the mouth of a small river. It was one of a number of prosperous towns in the fertile region of Campania. Outside the towns, especially along the coast of the bay, were many villas and farming estates, often owned by wealthy Romans, who were attracted to this area by its pleasant climate and peaceful surroundings.

Campania and the Bay of Naples

The town itself covered 66 hectares (163 acres), and was surrounded by a wall. The wall had eleven towers and eight gates. Roads led out from these gates to the neighbouring towns of Herculaneum, Nola, Nuceria, Stabiae, and to the harbour. Two wide main streets, known nowadays as the Street of Shops and Stabiae Street, crossed near the centre of the town; a third main street ran parallel to the Street of Shops.

The other streets, most of them also running in straight lines, divided the town neatly into blocks. There is no evidence that the Pompeians used street names and a stranger visiting the town would have had to ask his way from the local people.

Junction of two narrow streets in Pompeii

The streets, constructed of volcanic stone, had high pavements
on one or both sides to enable pedestrians to keep out of the rubbish
and avoid the traffic of wagons, horses and mules. Stepping-stones
provided convenient crossing places. Public water-fountains stood
at many street corners. The town's water-supply was brought from
the hills by an aqueduct; on reaching Pompeii it was stored in large
tanks on high ground at the northern side. The pressure created by
the water in these tanks provided a good flow through underground
lead pipes to all parts of the town, including the three sets of public
baths. Although most people drew their water from the public
fountains, the wealthier citizens paid special rates which allowed
them to take a private supply from the public pipes straight into
their homes.

In all the main streets there were bakers' shops and bars where hot and cold drinks and snacks could be bought. The main shopping areas were in the forum and along the Street of Shops north-east of the Stabian baths.

Ground plan of Pompeii

Carved or painted signs indicated different kinds of shop. The figures of two men carrying a large jar between them announced a wine merchant; a figure of a goat announced a dairy; a hammer and chisel, a stonemason. General advertisements and public notices were painted on the whitewashed walls outside shops and houses. We can still see notices advertising shows in the amphitheatre and political slogans supporting candidates at the last election.

A wine-seller's shop sign

At the western end of the town was the forum. This large open space, with a covered colonnade on three sides, was the centre for business and local government.

There were two theatres. Popular shows for large audiences were performed in the big open-air theatre, which could hold about 5,000 people, while the smaller one, which was roofed, was used for concerts and for other shows. At the eastern end of the town was a huge sports ground or 'palaestra', and next to it an amphitheatre in which gladiatorial combats and wild-animal hunts were staged. This amphitheatre was large enough to seat every inhabitant in Pompeii and visitors from neighbouring towns as well.

Like a modern seaport, Pompeii was a place where people of many nationalities were to be seen: Romans, Greeks, Syrians, Jews, Africans, Spaniards and probably several other nationalities as well, with their different languages and different religions. This regular coming and going of people, many of whom were merchants and businessmen, was made possible by the peaceful conditions that existed throughout the Roman empire at this time.

From Britain in the north-west to Syria and Palestine in the east, Rome maintained peace and provided firm government. The frontiers of the empire were held secure by Roman troops stationed at important points. Travel was made easy by a system of well-built roads; ships carried foodstuffs and luxury goods across the Mediterranean; taxes were collected in the provinces and the wealth of Rome increased. Pompeii was only a medium-sized town but played its part in the flourishing commercial life of the empire.

Shop sign over the door of a dairy

Words and phrases checklist

You have now met the following words three times or more. Check
that you are able to translate them.

ad	to
bibit	drinks
circumspectat	looks round
clāmat	shouts
ecce !	see ! look !
et	and
exit	goes out
exspectat	waits for
forum	forum
iānua	door
īrātus	angry
leō	lion
magnus	big
nāvis	ship
nōn	not
portat	carries
respondet	replies
rīdet	laughs, smiles
salvē !	hello !
surgit	gets up, rises
taberna	shop, inn
videt	sees
vīlla	house
vīnum	wine

in forō

Grumiō: ego sum coquus.
ego cēnam coquō.

Caecilius: ego sum argentārius.
ego pecūniam habeō.

Pantagathus: ego sum tōnsor.
ego barbam
tondeō.

Syphāx: ego sum vēnālīcius.
        ego servum vēndō.

poēta: ego sum poēta.
      ego versum recitō.

Celer: ego sum pictor.
     ego leōnem pingō.

Quīntus: quid tū coquis ?
Grumiō: ego cēnam coquō.

Quīntus: quid tū habēs ?
mercātor: ego pecūniam
        habeō.

Quīntus: quid tū tondēs ?
tōnsor: ego barbam tondeō.

Quīntus: quid tū vēndis ?
vēnālīcius: ego servum vēndō.

Quīntus: quid tū recitās ?
poēta: ego versum recitō.

Quīntus: quid tū pingis ?
pictor: ego leōnem pingō.

Metella: quis es tū ?
ancilla: ego sum Melissa.

Metella: quis es tū ?
vēnālīcius: ego sum Syphāx.

Metella: quis es tū ?
servus: ego sum Clēmēns.

Hermogenēs

Caecilius est in forō. Caecilius in forō argentāriam habet. Hermogenēs ad forum venit. Hermogenēs est mercātor Graecus. mercātor
Caecilium salūtat.

    'ego sum mercātor Graecus', inquit Hermogenēs. 'ego sum mer-
cātor probus. ego pecūniam quaerō.'   5
    'cūr tū pecūniam quaeris ?' inquit Caecilius.
    'ego nāvem habeō', respondet Hermogenēs. 'sed nāvis nōn adest;
nāvis est in Graeciā. ego tamen sum probus. ego semper pecūniam
reddō.'
    'ecce !' inquit Caecilius. 'ego cēram habeō. tū ānulum habēs ?'   10
    'ego ānulum habeō', respondet Hermogenēs. 'ānulus signum
habet. ecce ! ego signum in cērā imprimō.'
    Caecilius pecūniam trādit. mercātor pecūniam capit et ē forō
currit.
    ēheu ! Hermogenēs nōn revenit. mercātor pecūniam nōn reddit.   15
Caecilius Hermogenem ad basilicam vocat.

Words and phrases

argentāriam	banker's stall	cēram	wax tablet
Graecus	Greek	ānulum	ring
probus	honest	signum	seal, sign
cūr ?	why ?	ego imprimō	I press
nōn adest	is not here	trādit	hands over
in Graeciā	in Greece	capit	takes
tamen	however	currit	runs
semper	always	ad basilicam	to the law court
ego reddō	I give back		

in basilicā

iūdex basilicam intrat.

iūdex:	quis es tū ?
Caecilius:	ego sum Lūcius Caecilius Iūcundus.
iūdex:	tū es Pompēiānus ?
Caecilius:	ego sum Pompēiānus.
iūdex:	quid tū in urbe agis ?
Caecilius:	ego cotīdiē ad forum veniō. ego sum argentārius.
iūdex:	cūr tū hodiē ad basilicam venīs ?
Caecilius:	Hermogenēs multam pecūniam dēbet. Hermogenēs pecūniam nōn reddit.
Hermogenēs:	Caecilius est mendāx !
iūdex:	quis es tū ?
Hermogenēs:	ego sum Hermogenēs.
iūdex:	Hermogenēs, quid tū in urbe agis ?
Hermogenēs:	ego in forō negōtium agō. ego sum mercātor.
iūdex:	quid tū respondēs ? tū pecūniam dēbēs ?
Hermogenēs:	ego pecūniam nōn dēbeō. amīcus meus est testis.
amīcus:	ego sum testis. Hermogenēs pecūniam nōn dēbet. Caecilius est mendāx.
Caecilius:	tū, Hermogenēs, es mendāx. amīcus tuus quoque est mendāx. tū pecūniam nōn reddis . . .
iūdex:	satis ! tū Hermogenem accūsās, sed tū rem nōn probās.
Caecilius:	ego cēram habeō. tū signum in cērā vidēs.
Hermogenēs:	ēheu !
iūdex:	Hermogenēs, tū ānulum habēs ?
Caecilius:	ecce ! Hermogenēs ānulum cēlat.
iūdex:	ubi est ānulus ? ecce ! ānulus rem probat. ego Hermogenem convincō.

5

10

15

20

25

Words and phrases

iūdex	judge	meus	my, mine
quis ?	who ?	testis	witness
Pompēiānus	a citizen of Pompeii	tuus	your
quid tū agis ?	what do you do ?	tū accūsās	you accuse
in urbe	in the city	tū rem nōn ⎱	⎰ you do not prove
cotīdiē	every day	probās ⎰	⎱ the case
hodiē	today	cēlat	is hiding
dēbet	owes	ubi ?	where ?
mendāx	liar	ego convincō	I convict,
ego negōtium ⎱ ⎰ I work, I do			I find guilty
agō ⎰ ⎱ business			

About the language

1 In the first three Stages, you met sentences like this:

servus currit.   The slave runs.
ancilla ambulat.   The slave-girl walks.
mercātor sedet.   The merchant sits.

2 In Stage 4, you have met sentences with 'I' and 'you':

ego currō.	I run.	tū curris.	You run.
ego ambulō.	I walk.	tū ambulās.	You walk.
ego sedeō.	I sit.	tū sedēs	You sit.

3 Notice the three different forms of each word:

ego currō	tū curris	servus currit
ego ambulō	tū ambulās	ancilla ambulat
ego sedeō	tū sedēs	mercātor sedet

Notice also that the words 'ego' and 'tū' are not strictly necessary, since the endings '-ō' and '-s' make it clear that 'I' and 'you' are being spoken about. The Romans usually left out 'ego' and 'tū'.

4 The following example is rather different:

ego sum īrātus.　　I am angry.
tū es īrātus.　　You are angry.
servus est īrātus.　　The slave is angry.

5 Study and translate the following sentences:

1 Caecilius recitat. ego recitō.
2 Quīntus dormit. tū dormīs.
3 tū labōrās. servus labōrat.
4 Syphāx servum habet. ego servum habeō.
5 ego pecūniam trādō. tū pecūniam trādis.
6 Pantagathus est tōnsor. tū es mercātor. ego sum poēta.
7 ambulō; circumspectō; circumspectās.
8 audiō; audīs; habēs.

Practising the language

1 Complete each pair of sentences with a suitable word, choosing your answer from the words in brackets, and then translate them into English.

for example:　　ego sum argentārius.
　　　　　　　ego pecūniam . . . . . . (habeō, salūtō)

　　　　　　　ego sum argentārius.
　　　　　　　ego pecūniam habeō.

　　　　　　　I am a banker.
　　　　　　　I have money.

1 ego sum mercātor.
　ego nāvem . . . . . . (stō, habeō)
2 ego sum coquus.
　ego cēnam . . . . . . (dormiō, coquō)
3 ego sum Herculēs.
　ego fūstem . . . . . . (teneō, sedeō)

4 ego sum servus.

    ego in culīnā. . . . . . (habeō, labōrō)

5 tū es amīcus.

    tū vīllam. . . . . . (intrās, dūcis)

6 tū es ancilla.

    tū suāviter. . . . . . (venīs, cantās)

7 tū es mendāx.

    tū pecūniam. . . . . . (dēbēs, ambulās)

8 tū es iūdex.

    tū Hermogenem. . . . . . . (curris, convincis)

9 ego sum Syphāx.

    ego ancillam. . . . . . . (vēndō, ambulō)

10 tū es senex.

    tū in tabernā. . . . . . . (tenēs, sedēs)

2   Translate into English:

Celer in vīllā labōrat. Celer pictūram in triclīniō pingit. magnus leō
est in pictūrā. Celer ē vīllā discēdit.

    Grumiō ē tabernā revenit et vīllam intrat. Grumiō est ēbrius.
Grumiō pictūram videt. Grumiō est perterritus.

    'ēheu !' inquit Grumiō. 'leō est in triclīniō. leō mē spectat. leō mē   5
ferōciter petit.'

    Grumiō ē triclīniō currit et culīnam intrat. Clēmēns est in culīnā.
Clēmēns Grumiōnem spectat.

    'cūr tū es perterritus ?' inquit Clēmēns.

    'ēheu ! leō est in triclīniō', inquit Grumiō.   10

    'ita vērō', respondet Clēmēns, 'et servus ēbrius est in culīnā.'

discēdit	departs, leaves
ē tabernā	from the inn
ēbrius	drunk
ita vērō	yes

The forum

The forum was the civic centre and the heart of the business life of Pompeii. It was a large open space surrounded on three sides by a colonnade, with various important public buildings grouped closely round it. The open area, 143 metres (156 yards) long and 38 metres (42 yards) wide, was paved with stone. In it stood a number of statues commemorating the emperor, members of the emperor's family, and local citizens who had given distinguished service to the town.

The illustration below shows a typical scene in the forum. The trader on the left has set up his wooden stall and is selling small articles of ironware, pincers, knives and hammers; the trader on the right is a shoemaker. He has seated his customers on stools while he shows them his goods. Behind the traders is the colonnade. This elegant structure, supported by columns of white marble, provided an open corridor in which people could walk and do business out of the heat of the sun in the summer and protected from the rain in winter.

On the right of the same drawing are two statues of important citizens mounted on horseback. Behind them is one of the bronze gates through which people entered the forum. Wheeled traffic was not allowed to enter this commercial area. The whole forum was a pedestrian precinct and a row of upright stones at each entrance made an effective barrier.

In the drawing above, you see a public notice board fixed across the pedestals of three statues, and two people studying the notices. There were no newspapers in Pompeii, but certain kinds of information, such as election results and dates of processions and shows, had to be publicised. This was done by painting notices on the outside walls of various buildings and by putting up notice boards in the forum.

In addition to official announcements, thousands of casual scribblings were made on the walls by ordinary people recording lost property, accommodation to let, lovers' messages and witty remarks. One of these notices says,

'A bronze jar has been lost from this shop. A reward is offered for its recovery.'

Another complains of noise at night and asks the 'aedile' (the official who was responsible for law and order) to do something about it:

'Macerior requests the aedile to stop people from making a noise in the streets and disturbing decent folk who are asleep.'

Some of the most important public buildings were situated round the forum. In a prominent position at the north end stood the temple of Jupiter, the greatest of the Roman gods. It was probably from the steps of this temple that political speeches were made at

Ground plan of the forum

1 Temple of Jupiter
2 Temple of Apollo
3 Basilica
4 Temple of Venus
5 Offices
6 Statues
7 Guildhall of the cloth
  trade
8 Temple of the emperors
9 Temple of the lares of
  Pompeii
10 Market hall
11 Baths

election times. The temple of Apollo lay just to the south, and nearby was a public weights and measures table. At the south-west corner stood the 'basilica', or law court. This was a large, long building with rows of pillars inside and a high platform at one end on which the two senior officials, called 'duovirī', sat when hearing lawsuits. The basilica was also used as a meeting-place for business-men. South-west of the basilica was the temple of Venus, an impor-tant goddess for the Pompeians who believed she took a special interest in their town.

Along the south side of the forum were three offices in which the town council conducted its business. On the east side was the guildhall of the cloth trade. As this was one of the most prosperous industries in the town, it is not surprising that its headquarters were large and occupied such a prominent site. Next to it stood a temple in honour of the Roman emperors, and by the side of that a temple dedicated to the 'larēs', or guardian spirits of Pompeii. We have now mentioned five religious shrines around or near the forum. There were many others elsewhere in the town, including a temple of Isis, an Egyptian goddess, whose worship had been brought to Italy. In addition to these public shrines, each home had its own gods, called 'the lares and penates'. It is not easy for us to under-stand clearly the beliefs of the Pompeians about their gods; but perhaps the first point to keep in mind is that it seemed to them quite natural to believe in many gods rather than one. Different gods cared for different parts of human life. Apollo, for example, was concerned with law, medicine and music; Venus was the goddess of love and beauty.

In the north-east corner of the forum was a large covered market which contained permanent shops rather than temporary stalls. The traders here sold mainly meat, fish and vegetables. North-west of the market, just behind the temple of Jupiter, stood a set of public baths.

Business, religion, local government: these were the official purposes of the forum and its surrounding buildings. This great crowded square was the centre of much of the open-air life in Pompeii. Here people gathered to do business, to shop, or just to stroll and gossip with their friends.

Words and phrases checklist

agit	does
negōtium agit	does business
ānulus	ring
cēra	wax, wax tablet
coquit	cooks
cūr ?	why ?
ē	from, out of
ego	I
ēheu !	alas !
habet	has
inquit	says
iūdex	judge
mendāx	liar
pecūnia	money
perterritus	terrified
poēta	poet
quaerit	searches for, looks for
quis ?	who ?
reddit	gives back
satis	enough
sed	but
signum	sign, seal
tū	you
vēndit	sells
vocat	calls

in theātrō

in viā

canis est in viā.

canēs sunt in viā.

servus est in viā.

servī sunt in viā.

puella est in viā.

puellae sunt in viā.

puer est in viā.

puerī sunt in viā.

mercātor est in viā.

mercātōrēs sunt in viā.

in theātrō

spectātor in theātrō sedet.

spectātōrēs in theātrō sedent.

āctor in scaenā stat.

āctōrēs in scaenā stant.

fēmina spectat.

fēminae spectant.

senex dormit.

senēs dormiunt.

iuvenis plaudit.

iuvenēs plaudunt.

āctōrēs

magna turba est in urbe. fēminae et puellae sunt in turbā. senēs
quoque et iuvenēs sunt in turbā. servī hodiē nōn labōrant. senēs
hodiē nōn dormiunt. mercātōrēs hodiē nōn sunt occupātī. Pompēiānī sunt ōtiōsī. urbs tamen nōn est quiēta. Pompēiānī ad theātrum contendunt. magnus clāmor est in urbe.   5

   agricolae urbem intrant. nautae urbem petunt. pāstōrēs dē
monte veniunt et ad urbem contendunt. turba per portam ruit.

   nūntius in forō clāmat: 'āctōrēs sunt in urbe. āctōrēs sunt in
theātrō. Priscus fābulam dat. Priscus fābulam optimam dat. āctōrēs
sunt Actius et Sorex.'   10

   Caecilius et Metella ē vīllā discēdunt. argentārius et uxor ad
theātrum ambulant. Clēmēns et Melissa ad theātrum contendunt.
sed Grumiō in vīllā manet.

Words and phrases

āctōrēs	actors
turba	crowd
fēminae	women
puellae	girls
iuvenēs	young men
ōtiōsī	on holiday, idle
quiēta	quiet
ad theātrum	to the theatre
contendunt	hurry
clāmor	shout, uproar
agricolae	farmers
nautae	sailors
petunt	make for, seek
pāstōrēs	shepherds
dē monte	down from the mountain
per portam ruit	rushes through the gate
nūntius	messenger
fābulam dat	is putting on a play
uxor	wife
manet	remains, stays

Poppaea

Poppaea est ancilla. ancilla prope iānuam stat. ancilla viam spectat. dominus in hortō dormit. dominus est Lucriō. Lucriō est senex.

Poppaea: ego amīcum meum exspectō. ubi est amīcus ?
  (Lucriō stertit.)
  ēheu ! Lucriō est in vīllā.   5
  (agricolae in viā clāmant.)
agricolae: euge ! agricolae hodiē nōn labōrant !
Poppaea: Lucriō ! Lucriō ! agricolae urbem intrant. agricolae
  adsunt.
Lucriō: *(sēmisomnus)*   a . . . a . . . agricolae ?   10
puerī: euge ! Sorex ! Actius ! āctōrēs adsunt.
Poppaea: Lucriō ! Lucriō ! puerī per viam currunt.
Lucriō: quid tū clāmās, Poppaea ? cūr tū clāmōrem facis ?
Poppaea: Lucriō, Pompēiānī clāmōrem faciunt. agricolae et
  puerī sunt in viā.   15
Lucriō: cūr tū mē vexās ?
Poppaea: āctōrēs in theātrō fābulam agunt.
Lucriō: āctōrēs ?
Poppaea: Sorex et Actius adsunt.
Lucriō: quid tū dīcis ?   20
Poppaea: *(īrāta)* senēs ad theātrum ambulant, iuvenēs ad theāt-
  rum contendunt, omnēs Pompēiānī ad theātrum ruunt.

Words and phrases

euge !	hurray !	tū vexās	you annoy
adsunt	are here	fābulam agunt	act a play
sēmisomnus	half-asleep	tū dīcis	you say
puerī	boys	omnēs	all
tū clāmōrem facis	} { you make a noise		

āctōrēs in theātrō fābulam agunt.

Lucriō: euge ! āctōrēs adsunt. ego quoque ad theātrum contendō.
           (exit Lucriō. amīcus vīllam intrat.)   25
amīcus: salvē ! mea columba !
Poppaea: Grumiō, dēliciae meae ! salvē !
Grumiō: ubi est dominus tuus ?
Poppaea: Lucriō abest.
Grumiō: euge !   30

Words and phrases

mea columba   my dove   abest   is out
dēliciae meae   my darling

About the language

1 In the first four Stages, you have met sentences like these:

servus labōrat.   leō currit.
The slave works.   The lion runs.

puella sedet.   mercātor dormit.
The girl sits.   The merchant sleeps.

Sentences like these refer to *one* person or thing, and the form of
the words is said to be *singular*.

2 Sentences which refer to *more* than one person or thing use a different form of the words, known as the *plural*. Compare the singular and plural forms in the following sentences:

singular	*plural*
servus labōrat.	servī labōrant.
The slave works.	The slaves work.
puella sedet.	puellae sedent.
The girl sits.	The girls sit.
leō currit.	leōnēs currunt.
The lion runs.	The lions run.
mercātor dormit.	mercātōrēs dormiunt.
The merchant sleeps.	The merchants sleep.

Notice that in each of these sentences *both* words show the difference between singular and plural.

3 Study and translate the following sentences:

1 amīcus ambulat. amīcī ambulant.
2 āctor clāmat. āctōrēs clāmant.
3 senēs dormiunt. senex dormit.
4 vēnālīciī intrant. vēnālīcius intrat.
5 ancilla respondet. ancillae respondent.

4 Notice the difference between 'is' and 'are' in Latin:

mercātor est in viā.	mercātōrēs sunt in viā.
The merchant is in	The merchants are in
the street.	the street.

Practising the language

1 Complete each sentence with the right word. Write out the completed sentence in Latin and then translate it.

for example: senēs . . . . . . (dormit, dormiunt)
                          senēs dormiunt.
                          The old men are sleeping.

1 āctōrēs . . . . . . (adest, adsunt)
2 puellae in theātrō . . . . . . (sedent, sedet)
3 agricolae ad urbem . . . . . . (currunt, currit)
4 Pompēiānī clāmōrem . . . . . . (facit, faciunt)
5 servī ad theātrum . . . . . . (contendit, contendunt)

2 Complete each sentence with the right word. Write out the completed sentence in Latin and then translate it.

for example: mercātōrēs Caecilium . . . . . (quaerit, quaerunt)
                          mercātōrēs Caecilium quaerunt.
                          The merchants are looking for Caecilius.

1 pāstōrēs ad theātrum . . . . . . (contendit, contendunt)
2 pāstor pecūniam nōn . . . . . . (habet, habent)
3 puella āctōrem . . . . . . (laudat, laudant)
4 fēminae fābulam . . . . . . (spectat, spectant)
5 vēnālīciī ad urbem . . . . . . (venit, veniunt)
6 nūntius in forō . . . . . . (clāmat, clāmant)
7 senēs in forō . . . . . . (dormit, dormiunt)
8 pater . . . . . . in tablīnō. (est, sunt)

3   Translate into English:

hodiē Pompēiānī sunt ōtiōsī. dominī et servī nōn labōrant. multī
Pompēiānī in theātrō sedent. spectātōrēs Actium exspectant.
tandem Actius in scaenā stat. Pompēiānī plaudunt.

subitō Pompēiānī magnum clāmōrem audiunt. servus theātrum intrat. 'euge! fūnambulus adest', clāmat servus. Pompēi- 5
ānī Actium nōn spectant. omnēs Pompēiānī ē theātrō currunt et
fūnambulum spectant.

nēmō in theātrō manet. Actius tamen nōn est īrātus. Actius
quoque fūnambulum spectat.

multī	many	plaudunt	applaud, clap
spectātōrēs	spectators	fūnambulus	tight-rope walker
tandem	at last	nēmō	no one
scaenā	stage		

About the language

1   Study the following examples of singular and plural forms:

singular	*plural*
servus ambulat.	**servī** ambulant.
The slave walks.	The slaves walk.
puella rīdet.	**puellae** rīdent.
The girl smiles.	The girls smile.
mercātor contendit.	**mercātōrēs** contendunt.
The merchant hurries.	The merchants hurry.

2   Each of the words in heavy print is in the *nominative* case,
because it refers to a person or people who are performing some
action, such as walking or smiling.

3   'servus', 'puella' and 'mercātor' are therefore *nominative
singular* and 'servī', 'puellae' and 'mercātōrēs' are
nominative plural.

The theatre at Pompeii

Plays were not performed in Pompeii every day but only at festivals, which were held several times a year. When the notices appeared announcing a performance, there was great excitement in the town. On the day itself the shops were closed and no business was done in the forum. People set off for the theatre early in the morning. Men, women and slaves flocked through the streets, some carrying cushions, because the seats were made of stone, many taking food and drink for the day. The only people who did not need to hurry were the town councillors and other important citizens, for whom the best seats at the front of the auditorium were reserved. These important people carried tickets which indicated the entrance they should use and where they were to sit. The tickets were made of bone or ivory and were often decorated with engravings of the theatre, actors' masks, fruit or animals. Late-comers among the ordinary citizens had to be content with a seat right at the top of the large semicircular auditorium. The large theatre at Pompeii could hold 5,000 people.

A dramatic performance was a public occasion, and admission to the theatre was free. All the expenses were paid by a wealthy citizen, who provided the actors, the producer, the scenery and costumes. He volunteered to do this, not only to benefit his fellow-citizens, but also to gain popularity which would be useful in local political elections.

The performance consisted of a series of plays and lasted all day, even during the heat of the afternoon. To keep the spectators cool, a large canvas awning was suspended by ropes and pulleys across most of the theatre. The awning was managed by sailors, who were used to handling ropes and canvas; even so, on a windy day the awning could not be unfurled, and the audience had to make use of hats or sunshades to protect themselves from the sun. Between plays, scented water was sprinkled by attendants.

One of the most popular kinds of production was the 'pantomime', a mixture of opera and ballet. The plot, which was usually serious, was taken from the Greek myths. The parts of the different characters were mimed and danced by one masked performer, while a chorus sang the lyrics. An orchestra containing such instruments as the lyre, double pipes, trumpet and castanets accompanied the performance, providing a rhythmical beat. Pantomime actors were usually Greek slaves or freedmen. They were much admired for their skill and stamina, and attracted a large following of fans.

Equally popular were the comic actors, who played in vulgar farces about everyday life. The bronze statue of a comic actor, Sorex, was discovered at Pompeii, together with scribblings on walls naming other popular actors. One of these reads:

'Actius, our favourite, come back quickly.'

Actor playing the part of a slave sitting on an altar

Comic actors also appeared in the short one-act plays which were often put on at the end of longer performances. These short plays were about Italian country life and were packed with rude jokes and horseplay. They used just a few familiar characters, such as Pappus, an old fool, and Manducus, a greedy clown. These characters were instantly recognisable from the strange masks worn by the actors. The Roman poet, Juvenal, describes a performance of a play of this kind in a country theatre, where the children sitting on their

Scene from comedy. A young man returning drunk from a party is met by his angry father

mothers' laps shrank back in horror when they saw the gaping, white masks. These masks, like those used in other plays, were probably made of linen which was covered with plaster and painted.

Sometimes, at a festival, the old comedies of Plautus and Terence were put on. These plays also used a number of familiar characters, but the plots were complicated and the dialogue more witty than that of the farces. There is usually a young man from a respectable family who is leading a wild and carefree life; he is often in debt and in love with a pretty but unsuitable slave-girl. His father, who is old-fashioned and disapproving, has to be kept in the dark by deception. The son is usually helped in this by a cunning slave, who gets himself and his young master in and out of trouble at great speed.

For example, in Plautus' play called the *Mostellaria (The Haunted House)*, a young man called Philolaches is having a very good time while his father is abroad. Philolaches has also borrowed a lot of money to buy the freedom of the slave-girl he loves. One day he is having a party with friends outside his house, when his slave Tranio interrupts the merry-making to announce that Philolaches' father has returned unexpectedly and will arrive from the harbour at any moment. Amid the general panic, Tranio has an idea. He hustles Philolaches and his friends into the house and locks the door. The father now arrives. Tranio greets him respectfully but pretends that it is dangerous for him to go into the house because it is haunted.

Unfortunately, at this moment a money-lender turns up to claim the money borrowed by Philolaches. Tranio thinks quickly and pretends that the money was borrowed to buy the house next door. Even when Philolaches' father meets the real owner of the house, Tranio manages to hide the truth for some time, but he is found out at last and jumps onto the top of an altar to escape punishment. All ends happily, however, when one of Philolaches' friends arrives and persuades the father to forgive his son. Even Tranio is forgiven.

Words and phrases checklist

adest	is here
adsunt	are here
agricola	farmer
ambulat	walks
audit	hears
clāmor	shout, uproar
contendit	hurries
currit	runs
euge !	hurray !
fābula	play, story
fābulam agit	acts a play
fēmina	woman
hodiē	today
iuvenis	young man
meus	my, mine
multus	much
multī	many
optimus	very good, excellent
petit	makes for, attacks
plaudit	applauds
puella	girl
senex	old man
spectat	looks at, watches
stat	stands
turba	crowd
ubi ?	where ?
urbs	city
venit	comes

Fēlīx

servī per viam ambulābant.

canis subitō lātrāvit.

Grumiō canem timēbat.

'pestis !' clāmāvit coquus.

Clēmēns erat fortis.

sed canis Clēmentem superāvit.

Quīntus per viam ambulābat.

iuvenis clāmōrem audīvit.

canis Clēmentem vexābat.

Quīntus canem pulsāvit.

servī erant laetī.

servī Quīntum laudāvērunt.

pugna

Clēmēns in forō ambulābat. turba maxima erat in forō. servī et ancillae cibum emēbant. multī pistōrēs pānem vēndēbant. poēta recitābat. mercātor Graecus contentiōnem cum agricolā habēbat. mercātor īrātus pecūniam postulābat. subitō agricola Graecum pulsāvit, quod Graecus agricolam vituperābat. Pompēiānī rīdē-   5
bant, et agricolam incitābant. Clēmēns, postquam clāmōrem audī-vit, ad pugnam festīnāvit. tandem agricola mercātōrem superāvit et ē forō agitāvit. Pompēiānī agricolam fortem laudāvērunt.

Words and phrases

pugna	fight
maxima	very large
pistōrēs	bakers
pānem vēndēbant	were selling bread
contentiōnem habēbat	was having an argument
cum agricolā	with a farmer
postulābat	was demanding
subitō	suddenly
pulsāvit	hit, punched
quod	because
incitābant	were urging on
postquam	when, after
festīnāvit	hurried
superāvit	overpowered
agitāvit	chased

Fēlīx

multī Pompēiānī in tabernā vīnum bibēbant. Clēmēns tabernam
intrāvit. subitō Clēmēns 'Fēlīx !' clāmāvit. Clēmēns Fēlīcem laetē
salūtāvit. Fēlīx erat lībertus.

   Clēmēns Fēlīcem ad vīllam invītāvit. Clēmēns et Fēlīx vīllam
intrāvērunt. Clēmēns Caecilium et Metellam quaesīvit. Caecilius in   5
tablīnō scrībēbat. Metella in hortō sedēbat. Caecilius et Metella ad
ātrium festīnāvērunt et Fēlīcem salūtāvērunt. postquam Quīntus
ātrium intrāvit, Fēlīx iuvenem spectāvit. lībertus erat valdē com-
mōtus. paene lacrimābat; sed rīdēbat.

   tum Clēmēns ad culīnam festīnāvit. Grumiō in culīnā dormiēbat.   10
Clēmēns coquum excitāvit et tōtam rem nārrāvit. coquus, quod erat
laetus, cēnam optimam parāvit.

Words and phrases

laetē	happily
lībertus	freedman
invītāvit	invited
valdē commōtus	very moved, very much affected
paene lacrimābat	was almost weeping
tum	then
excitāvit	aroused, woke up
tōtam rem	the whole story
nārrāvit	told
parāvit	prepared

Fēlīx et fūr

post cēnam Quīntus rogāvit, 'pater, cūr Fēlīx nunc est lībertus?
ōlim erat servus tuus.'
   tum pater tōtam rem nārrāvit.

Caecilius:	Fēlīx ōlim in tablīnō scrībēbat. Fēlīx erat sōlus.
	Clēmēns et Grumiō cibum in forō quaerēbant. 5
	Metella aberat, quod sorōrem vīsitābat.
Fēlīx:	pater tuus aberat, quod argentāriam in forō admi-
	nistrābat.
Caecilius:	nēmō erat in vīllā nisi Fēlīx et īnfāns. parvus īnfāns
	in cubiculō dormiēbat. subitō fūr per iānuam in- 10
	trāvit. fūr tacitē ātrium circumspectāvit; tacitē
	cubiculum intrāvit, ubi īnfāns erat. Fēlīx nihil
	audīvit, quod intentē labōrābat. fūr parvum īnfan-
	tem ē vīllā tacitē portābat. subitō īnfāns vāgīvit.
	Fēlīx, postquam clāmōrem audīvit, statim ē tablīnō 15
	festīnāvit.
	'furcifer!' clāmāvit Fēlīx īrātus, et fūrem ferōci-
	ter pulsāvit. Fēlīx fūrem paene necāvit. ita Fēlīx
	parvum īnfantem servāvit.
Fēlīx:	dominus, postquam rem audīvit, erat laetus et mē 20
	līberāvit. ego igitur sum lībertus.
Quīntus:	sed quis erat īnfāns?
Caecilius:	erat Quīntus!

Words and phrases

fūr	thief	in cubiculō	in a bedroom
post	after	tacitē	quietly
rogāvit	asked	ubi	where
nunc	now	nihil	nothing
ōlim	once, some time ago	portābat	began to carry
sōlus	alone	vāgīvit	cried, wailed
aberat	was out	statim	at once
sorōrem	sister	necāvit	killed
administrābat	was looking after	ita	in this way
nisi	except	servāvit	saved
īnfāns	child, baby	līberāvit	freed, set free
parvus	little	igitur	therefore, and so

About the language

1   The sentences in the first five Stages have all been in the *present tense*. Study the following examples:

present tense

singular   servus **labōrat.**   The slave works.
plural   servī **labōrant.**   The slaves work.

2   In Stage 6, you have met the *imperfect tense* and the *perfect tense*. Study the different endings of the two tenses and their English translation:

imperfect tense

singular   poēta **recitābat.**   A poet was reciting.
             Metella in hortō **sedēbat.**   Metella was sitting in the garden.

plural   Pompēiānī vīnum **bibēbant.**   The Pompeians were drinking wine.
             servī in forō **ambulābant.**   The slaves were walking in the forum.

perfect tense

singular   Clēmēns clāmōrem **audīvit.**   Clemens heard the uproar.
             coquus **intrāvit.**   The cook entered.

plural   amīcī Caecilium **salūtāvērunt.**   The friends greeted Caecilius.
             iuvenēs ad tabernam **festīnāvērunt.**   The young men hurried to an inn.

3 Compare the endings of the imperfect and perfect tenses with the present tense. Notice that in all three tenses the singular ends in '-t' and the plural in '-nt'.

4 Notice how Latin shows the difference between 'is', 'are' and 'was', 'were':

present	*imperfect*
Caecilius **est** in tablīnō.	Caecilius **erat** in forō.
Caecilius is in the study.	Caecilius was in the forum.
servī **sunt** in culīnā.	servī **erant** in viā.
The slaves are in the kitchen.	The slaves were in the street.

Practising the language

1   Read the following story, and then answer the questions at the
end. Write your answers in English.

---

avārus

---

duo fūrēs ōlim ad vīllam contendēbant. in vīllā mercātor habitābat.
mercātor erat senex et avārus. avārus multam pecūniam habēbat.
fūrēs, postquam vīllam intrāvērunt, ātrium circumspectāvērunt.
　　'avārus', inquit fūr, 'est sōlus. avārus servum nōn habet.'
　　tum fūrēs tablīnum intrāvērunt. avārus clāmāvit et ferōciter   5
pugnāvit, sed fūrēs senem facile superāvērunt.
　　'ubi est pecūnia, senex ?' rogāvit fūr.
　　'servus fidēlis pecūniam in cubiculō custōdit', inquit senex.
　　'tū servum fidēlem nōn habēs, quod avārus es', clāmāvit fūr. tum
fūrēs cubiculum petīvērunt.   10
　　'pecūniam videō', inquit fūr. fūrēs cubiculum intrāvērunt, ubi
pecūnia erat, et pecūniam intentē spectāvērunt. sed ēheu ! ingēns
serpēns in pecūniā iacēbat. fūrēs serpentem timēbant et ē vīllā
celeriter festīnāvērunt.
　　in vīllā avārus rīdēbat et serpentem laudābat.   15
　　'tū es optimus servus. numquam dormīs. pecūniam meam semper servās.'

Words and phrases

avārus	miser	custōdit	is guarding
duo	two	ingēns	huge
habitābat	was living	serpēns	snake
inquit	said	iacēbat	was lying
pugnāvit	fought	timēbant	were afraid of, feared
facile	easily	celeriter	quickly
fidēlis	faithful	numquam	never

Questions

1 How many thieves were there ?
2 What did the thieves do immediately after they had entered
  the house ?
3 Why did one of the thieves think the miser would be alone ?
4 Who won the fight and why ?
5 Where was the money ?
6 Why did the thieves run away ?
7 What did the miser think of the snake and why ?

2 Complete each sentence with the right word. Write out the
completed sentence in Latin and then translate it.

for example: . . . . . . in forō ambulābat. (servus, servī)
                  servus in forō ambulābat.
                  The slave was walking in the forum.

                  . . . . . . forum spectābant. (amīcus, amīcī)
                  amīcī forum spectābant.
                  The friends were looking at the forum.

1 . . . . . . per viam festīnābat. (lībertus, lībertī)
2 . . . . . . pecūniam portābant. (servus, servī)
3 . . . . . . ātrium circumspectāvit. (fūr, fūrēs)
4 . . . . . . clāmōrem audīvērunt. (mercātor, mercātōrēs)
5 . . . . . . fūrem superāvērunt. (puer, puerī)
6 . . . . . . ad urbem festīnāvit. (nauta, nautae)

Slaves and freedmen

Wherever you travelled in the Roman world, you would find people who were slaves, like Grumio, Clemens and Melissa. They belonged to a master or mistress, to whom they had to give complete obedience; they were not free to make decisions for themselves; they could not marry; nor could they own personal possessions or be protected by courts of law. The law, in fact, did not regard them as human beings, but as things that could be bought and sold, treated well or treated badly. These people carried out much of the hard manual work but they also took part in many skilled trades and occupations. They did not live separately from free people; many slaves would live in the same house as their master and occupy rooms in the rear part of the house. Slaves and free people could often be found working together.

The Romans and others who lived round the Mediterranean in Classical times regarded slavery as a normal and necessary part of life; even those who realised that it was not a natural thing made no serious effort to abolish it. Good masters showed kindness to their slaves by giving them decent living conditions, by taking care of them and sometimes by setting them free.

People usually became slaves as a result either of being taken prisoner during a time of war or of being captured by pirates; the children of slaves were born into slavery. They came from many different tribes and countries, Gaul and Britain, Spain and North Africa, Egypt, different parts of Greece and Asia Minor, Syria and Palestine. By the time of the Emperor Augustus at the beginning of the first century A.D., there were perhaps as many as three slaves for every five free citizens in Italy. Most families owned at least one or two; a merchant like Caecilius would have no fewer than a dozen in his house and many more working on his estates and in his businesses. Very wealthy men owned hundreds and sometimes even thousands of slaves. A man called Pedanius Secundus, who lived in Rome, kept four hundred in his house there; when one of them murdered him, they were all put to death, in spite of protests by the people of Rome.

Slaves were employed in all kinds of work. In the country, their life was rougher and harsher than in the cities. They worked on farms, on big cattle ranches in southern Italy, in the mines and on the building of roads and bridges. Some of the strongest slaves were bought for training as gladiators.

Two customers (sitting down), attended by a slave, are inspecting a piece of cloth. The salesman in the centre and his two assistants may also be slaves

In the towns, slaves were used for both unskilled and skilled work. They were cooks and gardeners, general servants, labourers in factories, secretaries, musicians, actors and entertainers. In the course of doing such jobs, they were regularly in touch with their masters and other free men; they moved freely about the streets of the towns, went shopping, visited temples and were also quite often present in the theatre and at shows in the amphitheatre. Foreign visitors to Rome and Italy were sometimes rather surprised that there was so little visible difference between a slave and a poor free man.

Some masters were cruel and brutal to their slaves; but others were kind and humane. Common sense usually prevented a master from treating his slaves too harshly, since only fit, well-cared-for slaves were likely to work efficiently. A slave who was a skilled craftsman, particularly one who was able to read and write, keep accounts and manage the work of a small shop, would have cost a large sum of money; and a Roman master was generally too prudent to waste an expensive possession through carelessness.

Not every slave remained in slavery until the end of his life. Freedom was sometimes given as a reward for particularly good service, sometimes as a sign of friendship and respect. Freedom was also very commonly given at the death of a master by a statement in his will. But the law laid down certain limits. For example, a slave could not be freed before he was thirty years old.

The act of freeing a slave was called 'manūmissiō'. This word is connected with two other words, 'manus' (hand) and 'mittō' (send), and means 'a sending out from the hand' or 'setting free from control'. Manumission was performed in several ways. One method, the oldest, took the form of a legal ceremony before a public official, such as a judge. A witness claimed that the slave did not really belong to the master at all; the master did not deny the claim; the slave's head was then touched with a rod and he was declared officially free. There were other simpler methods. A master might manumit his slave by declaring him free in the presence of friends at home or merely by inviting him to recline on the couch at dinner.

The ex-slave became a 'lībertus' (freedman). He now had the opportunity to make his own way in life, and possibly to become an important member of his community. He did not, however, receive all the privileges of a citizen who had been born free. He could not stand as a candidate in public elections, nor could he become a high-ranking officer in the army. It was common for a freedman to become one of the clientes of his former master; he would visit him regularly to pay his respects, usually at the start of the morning, and help and support him whenever he could. This connection between them is seen very clearly in the names taken by a freedman. Suppose that his slave-name had been Felix and his master had been Lucius Caecilius Iucundus. As soon as he became free, Felix would take some of the names of his former master and call himself Lucius Caecilius Felix.

Some freedmen continued to do the same work that they had previously done as slaves; others were set up in business by their former masters. Others became priests in the temples or servants of the town council; the council secretaries, messengers, town clerk and town crier were all probably freedmen. Some became very rich and powerful. Two freedmen at Pompeii, who were called the Vettii and were possibly brothers, owned a house which is one of the most magnificent in the town. The colourful paintings on its walls and the elegant marble fountains in the garden show clearly how prosperous the Vettii were. Another Pompeian freedman was the architect who designed the large theatre; another was the father of Lucius Caecilius Iucundus.

Words and phrases checklist

abest	is out, is absent
aberat	was out, was absent
avārus	miser
cubiculum	bedroom
emit	buys
ferōciter	fiercely
festīnat	hurries
fortis	brave
fūr	thief
īnfāns	child, baby
intentē	intently
lībertus	freedman, ex-slave
ōlim	once, some time ago
parvus	small
per	through
postquam	after
pulsat	hits, thumps
quod	because
rēs	thing
scrībit	writes
subitō	suddenly
superat	overcomes, overpowers
tum	then
tuus	your, yours
vituperat	blames, curses

cēna

amīcus Caecilium vīsitābat.
vīllam intrāvit.

Caecilius amīcum exspectābat.
amīcum salūtāvit.

amīcus cum Caeciliō cēnābat.
cēnam laudāvit.

amīcus pōculum īnspexit.
vīnum gustāvit.

amīcus pōculum hausit.
tum fābulam nārrāvit.

Caecilius plausit.
'euge !' dīxit.

amīcī optimum vīnum
bibērunt.
tandem surrēxērunt.

servī in ātriō stābant.
iānuam aperuērunt.

Caecilius et amīcus 'valē'
dīxērunt.
amīcus ē vīllā discessit.

fābula mīrābilis

multī amīcī cum Caeciliō cēnābant. Fēlīx quoque aderat. omnēs amīcī coquum laudāvērunt, quod cēna erat optima.

postquam omnēs cēnāvērunt,* Caecilius clāmāvit, 'ubi est Decēns ? Decēns nōn adest.' tum Caecilius Clēmentem ē vīllā mīsit. servus Decentem per urbem quaesīvit.   5

postquam servus ē vīllā discessit, Fēlīx pōculum hausit. tum lībertus fābulam mīrābilem nārrāvit:

'ōlim amīcus meus ex urbe discēdēbat. nox erat obscūra, quod lūna nōn lūcēbat. amīcus per viam festīnābat, ubi silva erat, et subitō centuriōnem cōnspexit. amīcus meus centuriōnem salūtāvit.   10 centuriō tamen nihil dīxit. tum centuriō tunicam dēposuit. ecce ! centuriō ēvānuit. ingēns lupus subitō appāruit. amīcus meus valdē timēbat. ingēns lupus ululāvit et ad silvam festīnāvit. tunica in viā iacēbat. amīcus tunicam cautē īnspexit. ecce ! tunica erat lapidea. tum amīcus rem intellēxit. ille centuriō erat versipellis.'   15

Words and phrases

fābula	story	dīxit	said
mīrābilis	marvellous, strange	tunicam	tunic
mīsit	sent	dēposuit	took off
discessit	departed, left	ēvānuit	vanished
pōculum hausit	drained his wine-cup	lupus	wolf
ex urbe	from the city	appāruit	appeared
nox	night	ululāvit	howled
obscūra	dark, gloomy	cautē	cautiously
lūna	moon	īnspexit	looked at, examined
nōn lūcēbat	was not shining	lapidea	made of stone
silva	wood	rem intellēxit	understood the truth
centuriōnem	centurion	ille centuriō	that centurion
cōnspexit	caught sight of	versipellis	werewolf

About the language

1 Study the following example:

mercātor Caecilium vīsitābat. mercātor vīllam intrāvit.
A merchant was visiting Caecilius. The merchant entered
the house.

2. In Stage 7, you have met a shorter way of saying this:

mercātor Caecilium vīsitābat. vīllam intrāvit.
A merchant was visiting Caecilius. He entered the house.

The following sentences behave in the same way:

amīcī cum Caeciliō cēnābant. coquum laudāvērunt.
Some friends were dining with Caecilius. They praised the
cook.

ancilla in ātriō stābat. dominum salūtāvit.
The slave-girl was standing in the hall. She greeted the master.

3 Further examples for study and translation:

1 Grumiō in culīnā labōrābat. cēnam parābat.
2 āctōrēs in theātrō clāmābant. fābulam agēbant.
3 Metella nōn erat in vīllā. in hortō ambulābat.
4 lībertī in tabernā bibēbant. Grumiōnem salūtāvērunt.
5 iuvenis pōculum hausit. vīnum laudāvit.

4 Notice that Latin does not usually include a separate word for
'he', 'she' or 'they'.

Decēns

postquam Fēlīx fābulam nārrāvit, omnēs plausērunt. tum omnēs tacēbant et aliam fābulam exspectābant. subitō Caecilius et hospitēs clāmōrem audīvērunt. omnēs ad ātrium festīnāvērunt, ubi Clēmēns stābat.

Caecilius:	hercle ! quid est ? cūr tū clāmōrem facis ?
Clēmēns:	Decēns, Decēns . . . 5
Caecilius:	quid est ?
Clēmēns:	Decēns est mortuus.
omnēs:	quid ? mortuus ? ēheu !
	(duo servī intrant.)
Caecilius:	quid dīcis ? 10
servus prīmus:	dominus meus ad vīllam tuam veniēbat; dominus gladiātōrem prope amphitheātrum cōnspexit.
servus secundus:	gladiātor dominum terruit, quod gladium ingentem vibrābat. tum gladiātor clāmāvit,
	'tū mē nōn terrēs, leō, tū mē nōn terrēs! leōnēs 15 amīcum meum in arēnā necāvērunt, sed tū mē nōn terrēs!'
	Decēns valdē timēbat.
	'tū es īnsānus', inquit dominus. 'ego nōn sum leō. sum homō.' 20
	gladiātor tamen dominum ferōciter petīvit et

Words and phrases

plausērunt	applauded	secundus	second
tacēbant	were silent	terruit	frightened
aliam	another	gladium	sword
hospitēs	guests	vibrābat	was brandishing,
hercle !	by Hercules !		was waving
mortuus	dead	in arēnā	in the arena
prīmus	first	īnsānus	mad, crazy
gladiātōrem	gladiator	homō	man
prope amphitheātrum }} {{	near the amphitheatre		

eum ad amphitheātrum trāxit. dominus perterritus
clāmāvit. Clēmēns clāmōrem audīvit. Clēmēns,
quod fortis erat, amphitheātrum intrāvit. Decentem in arēnā cōnspexit. dominus meus erat mor-   25
tuus.

Caecilius: ego rem intellegō! gladiātor erat Pugnāx. Pugnāx
erat gladiātor nōtissimus. Pugnāx ōlim in arēnā
pugnābat, et leō Pugnācem necāvit. Pugnāx nōn
vīvit; Pugnāx est umbra. umbra Decentem necā-   30
vit.

Words and phrases

eum	him	vīvit	is alive
trāxit	dragged	umbra	ghost
nōtissimus	very well known		

post cēnam

postquam Caecilius rem explicāvit, omnēs amīcī tacēbant. mox
amīcī 'valē' dīxērunt et ē vīllā discessērunt. per viam timidē prōcēdēbant. nūllae stēllae lūcēbant. nūlla lūna erat in caelō. amīcī
nihil audīvērunt, quod viae dēsertae erant. amīcī per urbem tacitē
prōcēdēbant, quod umbram timēbant.   5
    subitō fēlēs ululāvit. amīcī valdē timēbant. omnēs per urbem
perterritī ruērunt, quod dē vītā dēspērābant. clāmōrem mīrābilem
faciēbant. multī Pompēiānī erant sollicitī, quod clāmōrem audīvērunt. Caecilius tamen clāmōrem nōn audīvit, quod in cubiculō
dormiēbat.   10

Words and phrases

explicāvit	explained	dēsertae	deserted
valē	goodbye	fēlēs	cat
timidē	fearfully	ruērunt	rushed
prōcēdēbant	were advancing, were proceeding	dē vītā dēspērābant	were despairing for their life
nūllae stēllae	no stars	sollicitī	worried, anxious
in caelō	in the sky		

About the language

1   In Stage 6 you met examples of the perfect tense. They looked like this:

> senex ad tabernam **ambulāvit.**
> The old man walked to the inn.

2
> amīcī in urbe **dormīvērunt.**
> The friends slept in the city.

This is the commonest way in which Latin forms the perfect tense.

2   In Stage 7 you have met other common forms of the perfect tense. Compare them with their imperfect forms:

	imperfect	*perfect*
singular	appārēbat	appāruit
	he was appearing	he appeared
	dīcēbat	dīxit
	he was saying	he said
	discēdēbat	discessit
	he was departing	he departed
plural	appārēbant	appāruērunt
	they were appearing	they appeared
	dīcēbant	dīxērunt
	they were saying	they said
	discēdēbant	discessērunt
	they were departing	they departed

3   If you are not sure whether a particular word is in the present tense or the perfect tense, you can check by looking it up in the 'Words and phrases' section of the Language Information pamphlet.

Practising the language

1 Complete each sentence with the right phrase, and then translate it.

> for example: amīcī . . . . . .(vīllam intrāvit, cēnam laudāvērunt)
> amīcī cēnam laudāvērunt.
> The friends praised the dinner.

1 mercātor . . . . . (ē vīllā discessit, clāmōrem audīvērunt)
2 amīcī . . . . . (pōculum īnspexit, rem intellēxērunt)
3 leōnēs . . . . . (gladiātōrem terruit, gladiātōrem cōnspexērunt)
4 lībertī . . . . . (lūnam spectāvit, ad portum festīnāvērunt)
5 centuriō . . . . . (fābulam audīvit, servum laudāvērunt)
6 fūr . . . . (per urbem ruit, centuriōnem terruērunt)
7 Caecilius et amīcus . . . . . (leōnem cōnspexit, portum petīvērunt)
8 ancillae . . . . (ad vīllam ambulāvit, in vīllā dormīvērunt)

2 Complete each sentence with the right word, and then translate it.

> for example: . . . . . . cēnam parāvit. (coquus, coquum)
> coquus cēnam parāvit.
> The cook prepared the dinner.

1 Clēmēns . . . . . . excitāvit. (coquus, coquum)
2 . . . . . fābulam nārrāvit. (lībertus, lībertum)
3 . . . . . gladiātōrem cōnspexērunt. (amīcus, amīcī)
4 . . . . . ad forum festīnāvērunt. (agricola, agricolae)
5 ancilla . . . . . aperuit. (iānua, iānuam)
6 . . . . . clāmōrem audīvit. (poēta, poētae)
7 fūrēs . . . . . necāvērunt. (centuriō, centuriōnem).
8 . . . . . cēnam laudāvit. (gladiātor, gladiātōrem)
9 . . . . . cibum ad theātrum portāvērunt. (spectātor, spectātōrēs)
10 . . . . . ē vīllā discessit. (senex, senēs)

vēnātiō

Quīntus amīcum suum vīsitābat. amīcus erat Gāius. Gāius erat vir fortis et vēnātor. in vīllā magnificā habitābat. Quīntus, postquam ad hanc vīllam vēnit, ātrium intrāvit. pictūra pretiōsa et maxima erat in ātriō. vēnātōrēs et canēs et cervī erant in pictūrā. Gāius hanc pictūram amābat, quod pulcherrima erat.   5

postquam Quīntus amīcum salūtāvit, Gāius dīxit:

'tū opportūnē venīs. ingēns aper latet in monte Vesuviō. servī meī sunt ignāvī; aprum timent. num tū timēs?'

'aper est animal ferōx', respondit iuvenis. 'ego tamen nōn timeō.'

tum Quīntus longum vēnābulum cēpit et amīcī ad vēnātiōnem   10 contendērunt. multī servī et multī canēs aderant. omnēs ad montem prōcessērunt, ubi aper latēbat.

servī, postquam aprum vīdērunt, clāmōrem fēcērunt. aper ferōx, quod clāmōrem audīvit, impetum fēcit. Quīntus fortiter prōcessit et vēnābulum ēmīsit. ecce! aprum trānsfīxit. ingēns aper ad terram   15 mortuus dēcidit. multus sanguis ex ōre fluēbat.

Words and phrases

vēnātiō	hunt	animal	animal
suum	his	ferōx	ferocious
vir	man	longum	long
vēnātor	hunter	vēnābulum	hunting spear
magnificā	magnificent	cēpit	took
hanc	this	prōcessērunt	proceeded,
vēnit	came		advanced
pretiōsa	precious, expensive	vīdērunt	saw
cervī	deer	clāmōrem }	{ made a noise,
amābat	liked, loved	fēcērunt }	{ shouted
pulcherrima	very beautiful	impetum fēcit	made an attack,
opportūnē	just at the right time		charged
aper	boar	vēnābulum	
latet	lies hidden	ēmīsit	threw his spear
in monte }	{ on Mount	fortiter	bravely
Vesuviō }	{ Vesuvius	trānsfīxit	pierced
ignāvī	cowards	terram	ground
num tū }	{ surely *you* are	dēcidit	fell down
timēs? }	{ not afraid?	ex ōre	from its mouth

Metella et Melissa

Metella Melissam in vīllā quaerēbat. Metella culīnam intrāvit, ubi
Grumiō labōrābat. Grumiō erat īrātus.

'cūr tū es īrātus, Grumiō ? cūr ferōciter circumspectās ?' rogāvit
Metella.

'heri Melissa cēnam optimam parāvit', respondit coquus. 'hodiē   5
ego cēnam pessimam parō, quod nūllus cibus adest. heri multus
cibus erat in culīnā. ancilla omnem cibum coxit.'

Metella ē culīnā discessit et ad tablīnum festīnāvit, ubi Clēmēns
labōrābat. Clēmēns quoque erat īrātus.

'Melissa est pestis !' clāmāvit servus.   10

'quid fēcit Melissa ?' rogāvit Metella.

'heri Melissa in tablīnō labōrābat', respondit Clēmēns. 'hodiē
ego in tablīnō labōrō. ecce ! cērae et stilī absunt. nihil est in locō
propriō.'

Metella, postquam ē tablīnō discessit, hortum intrāvit. Metella   15
Melissam in hortō vīdit. ēheu ! ancilla lacrimābat.

'Melissa, cūr lacrimās ?' rogāvit Metella.

'lacrimō quod Grumiō et Clēmēns mē vituperant', respondit
ancilla.

'ego tamen tē nōn vituperō ', inquit Metella. 'ego tē laudō. ecce !   20
tū crīnēs meōs optimē compōnis. stolam meam optimē compōnis.
fortasse Grumiō et Clēmēns tē nōn laudant; sed ego tē laudō, quod
mē dīligenter cūrās.'

Words and phrases

heri	yesterday	crīnēs	hair
pessimam	very bad	optimē	very well
coxit	cooked	compōnis	arrange
stilī	pens	stolam	dress
	(used for writing	fortasse	perhaps
	on wax tablets)	dīligenter	carefully
in locō propriō	in the right place	cūrās	look after

About the language

1   Notice how the following words form their perfect tense. Compare their present and perfect forms.

present		*perfect*	
facit	faciunt	fēcit	fēcērunt
he makes	they make	he made	they made
capit	capiunt	cēpit	cēpērunt
he takes	they take	he took	they took

2   Compare this with the way some words behave in English:

I run	I ran
I give	I gave
I come	I came

Roman beliefs about life after death

The Romans did not place the tombs of the dead in a quiet, lonely place, but by the side of the road just outside the town, where they could be seen and admired by the passers-by. The tombs at Pompeii can still be seen along the roads that go north from the Herculaneum Gate and south from the Nuceria Gate.

Some were grand and impressive and looked like small houses; others were much more plain and simple. It was a common custom to decorate them with garlands of flowers and put offerings of food and wine before them.

In burying the dead along busy roads, and not in a peaceful cemetery, the Romans were not showing any lack of respect. On the contrary, they believed that unless the dead were properly buried and looked after, their ghosts would haunt the living and possibly do them harm. It was most important to provide a dead man with a tomb or grave, where his ghost could have a home. But it was also

Tombs outside the Nuceria Gate

thought that he would want to be close to the life of the living. One tomb has this inscription: 'I see and I gaze upon all who come from and to the city', and another, 'Lollius has been placed by the side of the road in order that all passers-by may say to him "Good day, Lollius".'

It was believed that the dead in some way continued the activities of life, and therefore had to be supplied with the things they would need. A hunter would want his spear, a farmer his farming tools, a woman her spindle. If the body of the dead person was buried, his possessions were buried with him; if he was cremated, they were burnt with him.

A Greek writer called Lucian tells the story of a husband who had burnt all his dead wife's jewellery and clothes on the funeral pyre, so that she might have them in the next world. A week later he was trying to comfort himself by reading a book about life after death, when the ghost of his wife appeared. She began to reproach him because he had not burnt one of her gilt sandals, which, she said, was lying under a chest. The family dog then barked and the ghost disappeared. The husband looked under the chest, found the sandal, and burnt it.

The ghosts of the dead were also thought to be hungry and thirsty, and therefore had to be given food and drink. Offerings of eggs, beans, lentils, flour and wine were placed regularly at the tomb. Sometimes holes were made in the tomb so that wine could be poured inside. Wine was offered because it was a convenient substitute for blood, the favourite drink of the dead. However, at the funeral and on special occasions animals were sacrificed, and their blood offered.

It was thought, however, that in spite of these attempts to look after them, the dead did not lead a very happy existence. In order to help them forget their unhappiness, their tombs were often decorated with flowers and surrounded by little gardens, a custom which has lasted to this day, although its original meaning has changed. With the same purpose in mind, the family and friends of a dead man held a banquet after the funeral and on the anniversary of his death. Sometimes these banquets took place in a dining-room attached to the tomb itself, sometimes in the family home. The ghosts of the dead were thought to attend and enjoy these cheerful occasions.

Some people also believed in an underworld where the wicked were punished for the misdeeds they had committed when alive and where the good lived happily for ever. Stories were told about the punishments suffered by famous evil-doers such as the wicked Tityus, who had his liver pecked out by vultures, and the daughters of Danaus, who were condemned to pour water for ever into jars that had holes in the bottom. In the first century A.D. most people did not take these stories seriously, but they continued to tell them to naughty children to make them behave themselves.

There were a few people who did not believe in any form of life after death. These were the followers of a Greek called Epicurus, who taught that, when a man died, the breath that gave him life dissolved into the air and was lost for ever. Men had therefore no need to fear the next world, and could devote all their energies to making the most of this one.

Words and phrases checklist

cēnat	dines
centuriō	centurion
cōnspicit	catches sight of
cum	with
facit	makes, does
heri	yesterday
ingēns	huge
intellegit	understands
lacrimat	weeps
mortuus	dead
nārrat	tells, relates
necat	kills
nihil	nothing
omnis	all
parat	prepares
pestis	pest
pōculum	wine-cup
prōcēdit	advances, proceeds
prope	near
pulcher	beautiful
rogat	asks
tacitē	quietly
tamen	however
terret	frightens
umbra	ghost
valdē	very much

gladiātōrēs

nūntiī spectāculum nūntiābant.
Pompēiānī nūntiōs audiēbant.

gladiātōrēs per viam
prōcēdēbant.
Pompēiānī gladiātōrēs
laudābant.

puellae iuvenēs salūtāvērunt.
iuvenēs quoque ad
amphitheātrum contendēbant.

servī fēminās spectābant, quod
fēminae ad spectāculum
contendēbant.

puerī per viam festīnābant.
puellae puerōs salūtāvērunt.

Pompēiānī tabernās nōn
intrābant, quod tabernae
erant clausae.

Pompēiānī gladiātōrēs intentē spectābant, quod gladiātōrēs in arēnā pugnābant.

postquam gladiātōrēs Pompēiānōs salūtāvērunt, Pompēiānī plausērunt.

spectātōrēs murmillōnēs incitābant, quod murmillōnēs saepe victōrēs erant.

gladiātōrēs

Rēgulus erat senātor Rōmānus. in vīllā magnificā habitābat. vīlla erat prope Nūceriam. Nūcerīnī et Pompēiānī erant inimīcī. Nūcerīnī, quod amphitheātrum nōn habēbant, saepe ad amphitheātrum Pompēiānum veniēbant; saepe erant turbulentī.

Rēgulus ōlim spectāculum splendidum in amphitheātrō ēdidit,   5
quod diem nātālem celebrābat. multī Nūcerīnī igitur ad urbem vēnērunt. cīvēs Pompēiānī erant īrātī, quod Nūcerīnī viās complēbant. omnēs tamen ad forum contendērunt, ubi nūntiī erant. nūntiī spectāculum optimum nūntiābant:

'gladiātōrēs adsunt! vīgintī gladiātōrēs hodiē pugnant! rētiāriī   10
adsunt! murmillōnēs adsunt! bēstiāriī bēstiās ferōcēs agitant!'

Pompēiānī, postquam nūntiōs audīvērunt, ad amphitheātrum quam celerrimē contendērunt. Nūcerīnī quoque ad amphitheātrum festīnāvērunt. multī Pompēiānī igitur nōn intrāvērunt. hī Pompēiānī Nūcerīnōs et Rēgulum vituperābant, quod tōta cavea plēna erat.   15
spectātōrēs tamen prīmam pugnam exspectābant.

Words and phrases

senātor Rōmānus	a Roman senator	complēbant	were filling
Nūcerīnī	the people of Nuceria	nūntiābant	were announcing
inimīcī	enemies		
saepe	often	vīgintī	twenty
turbulentī	rowdy, disorderly	bēstiāriī	beast-fighters
spectāculum	show, spectacle	bēstiās	beasts
splendidum	splendid	quam celerrimē	as quickly as possible
ēdidit	presented		
diem nātālem	birthday	hī	these
celebrābat	was celebrating	cavea	seating area
cīvēs	citizens	plēna	full

in arēnā

duo rētiāriī et duo murmillōnēs arēnam intrāvērunt. postquam gladiātōrēs spectātōrēs salūtāvērunt, tuba sonuit. tum gladiā- tōrēs pugnam commīsērunt. murmillōnēs Pompēiānōs valdē dēlectābant, quod saepe victōrēs erant. Pompēiānī igitur murmillōnēs incitābant. sed rētiāriī, quod erant expedītī, murmil- lōnēs facile ēvītāvērunt.   5

'rētiāriī nōn pugnant ! rētiāriī sunt ignāvī !' clāmāvērunt Pompēiānī. Nūcerīnī tamen respondērunt, 'rētiāriī sunt callidī ! rētiāriī murmillōnēs dēcipiunt !'

murmillōnēs rētiāriōs frūstrā ad pugnam prōvocāvērunt. tum   10 murmillō clāmāvit, 'ūnus murmillō facile duōs rētiāriōs superat.'

Pompēiānī plausērunt. tum murmillō rētiāriōs statim petīvit. murmillō et rētiāriī ferōciter pugnāvērunt. rētiāriī tandem murmillōnem graviter vulnerāvērunt. tum rētiāriī alterum murmillōnem petīvērunt. hic murmillō fortiter pugnāvit, sed   15 rētiāriī eum quoque superāvērunt.

Pompēiānī, quod īrātī erant, murmillōnēs vituperābant; missiōnem tamen postulābant, quod murmillōnēs fortēs erant. Nūcerīnī mortem postulābant. omnēs spectātōrēs tacēbant, et Rēgulum intentē spectābant. Rēgulus, quod Nūcerīnī mortem   20 postulābant, pollicem vertit. Pompēiānī erant īrātī, et vehementer clāmābant. rētiāriī tamen, postquam Rēgulus signum dedit, murmillōnēs interfēcērunt.

Words and phrases

tuba	trumpet
sonuit	sounded
pugnam	
commīsērunt	began the fight
victōrēs	victors, winners
expedītī	lightly armed
ēvītāvērunt	avoided
callidī	clever, cunning
dēcipiunt	are deceiving, are tricking
frūstrā	in vain
prōvocāvērunt	challenged
ūnus	one
graviter	seriously
vulnerāvērunt	wounded
alterum	the second
hic	this
missiōnem	release
mortem	death
pollicem vertit	turned his thumb up
vehementer	violently, loudly
dedit	gave
interfēcērunt	killed

About the language

1   From Stage 2 onwards, you have met sentences like these:

amīcus **puellam** salūtat.   The friend greets the girl.

dominus **servum** vituperābat.   The master was cursing the slave.

nautae **mercātōrem** laudāvērunt.   The sailors praised the merchant.

In each of these examples, the person who has something done to him or her, is indicated in Latin by the *accusative singular*.

2   In Stage 8, you have met sentences like these:

amīcus **puellās** salūtat.   The friend greets the girls.

dominus **servōs** vituperābat.   The master was cursing the slaves.

nautae **mercātōrēs** laudāvērunt.   The sailors praised the merchants.

In these examples, the people who have something done to them are indicated in Latin by the *accusative plural*.

3   You have now met the following forms:

singular		*plural*	
nominative	*accusative*	*nominative*	*accusative*
puella	puellam	puellae	puellās
servus	servum	servī	servōs
mercātor	mercātōrem	mercātōrēs	mercātōrēs
leō	leōnem	leōnēs	leōnēs

4   Further examples for study and translation:

1 agricola gladiātōrem laudāvit. agricola gladiātōrēs laudāvit.

2 servus agricolam interfēcit. servus agricolās interfēcit.

3 centuriō servōs laudāvit.

4 puer āctōrēs ad theātrum dūxit.

5 senex āctōrem ad forum dūxit.

6 amīcus fābulās nārrāvit.

7 amīcī ancillam salūtāvērunt.

8 agricolae nūntiōs audīvērunt.

When you have read this passage, answer the questions at the end.

vēnātiō

postquam rētiāriī ex arēnā discessērunt, tuba iterum sonuit. subitō
multī cervī arēnam intrāvērunt. cervī per tōtam arēnam currēbant,
quod perterritī erant. tum canēs ferōcēs per portam intrāvērunt.
canēs statim cervōs perterritōs agitāvērunt et interfēcērunt.
postquam canēs cervōs superāvērunt, lupī arēnam intrāvērunt.   5
lupī, quod valdē ēsuriēbant, canēs ferōciter petīvērunt. canēs
erant fortissimī, sed lupī facile canēs superāvērunt.

　　Nūcerīnī erant laetissimī et Rēgulum laudābant. Pompēiānī
tamen nōn erant contentī, sed clāmābant, 'ubi sunt leōnēs? cūr
Rēgulus aprōs et leōnēs retinet?'   10

　　Rēgulus, postquam hunc clāmōrem audīvit, signum dedit. statim
trēs leōnēs per portam ruērunt. tuba iterum sonuit. bēstiāriī arēnam
audācissimē intrāvērunt. leōnēs tamen bēstiāriōs nōn petīvērunt.
leōnēs in arēnā recubuērunt. leōnēs obdormīvērunt!

　　tum Pompēiānī erant īrātissimī, quod Rēgulus spectāculum   15
rīdiculum ēdēbat. Pompēiānī Rēgulum et Nūcerīnōs ex
amphitheātrō agitāvērunt. Nūcerīnī per viās fugiēbant, quod valdē
timēbant. Pompēiānī tamen gladiōs suōs dēstrīnxērunt et multōs
Nūcerīnōs interfēcērunt. ecce! sanguis nōn in arēnā sed per viās
fluēbat.   20

Words and phrases

iterum	again	obdormīvērunt	went to sleep
ēsuriēbant	were hungry	īrātissimī	very angry
fortissimī	very brave	rīdiculum	ridiculous, silly
retinet	is holding back	ēdēbat	was presenting
hunc	this	fugiēbant	began to flee
trēs	three	suōs	their
audācissimē	very boldly	dēstrīnxērunt	drew
recubuērunt	lay down		

Questions

1 What happened when the trumpet sounded ?
2 When did the wolves enter the arena ?
3 What was the attitude of the citizens of Pompeii to the first part of the show ?
4 What did Regulus do ?
5 What went wrong with the show ?
6 Why did the Pompeians attack the citizens of Nuceria ?
7 What made this riot so serious ?

pāstor et leō

ōlim pāstor in silvā ambulābat. subitō pāstor leōnem cōnspexit. leō tamen pāstōrem nōn agitāvit. leō lacrimābat ! pāstor, postquam leōnem cōnspexit, erat attonitus et rogāvit,

'cūr lacrimās, leō ? cūr mē nōn agitās ? cūr mē nōn cōnsūmis ?'

leō trīstis pedem ostendit. pāstor spīnam in pede cōnspexit,   5
tum clāmāvit,

'ego spīnam videō ! spīnam ingentem videō ! nunc intellegō ! tū lacrimās, quod pēs dolet.'

pāstor, quod benignus et fortis erat, ad leōnem cautē vēnit et spīnam īnspexit. leō fremuit, quod ignāvus erat.   10

'leō !' exclāmāvit pāstor, 'ego perterritus sum, quod tū fremis. sed tē adiuvō. ecce ! spīna !'

postquam hoc dīxit, pāstor spīnam quam celerrimē extrāxit. leō ignāvus iterum fremuit et ē silvā festīnāvit.

Words and phrases

attonitus	astonished	fremuit	roared
trīstis	sad	ignāvus	cowardly
pedem	foot, paw	exclāmāvit	shouted
ostendit	showed	adiuvō	help
spīnam	thorn	hoc	this
dolet	hurts	extrāxit	pulled out
benignus	kind		

posteā, Rōmānī hunc pāstōrem comprehendērunt, quod 15
Christiānus erat, et eum ad arēnam dūxērunt. postquam arēnam
intrāvit, pāstor spectātōrēs vīdit et valdē timēbat. tum pāstor
bēstiās vīdit et clāmāvit, 'nunc mortuus sum ! videō leōnēs et
lupōs. ēheu !'

tum ingēns leō ad eum ruit. leō, postquam pāstōrem olfēcit, nōn 20
eum cōnsūmpsit sed lambēbat ! pāstor attonitus leōnem agnōvit et
dīxit,

'tē agnōscō ! tū es leō trīstis ! spīna erat in pede tuō.'

leō iterum fremuit, et pāstōrem ex arēnā ad salūtem dūxit.

Words and phrases

posteā	afterwards	lambēbat	began to lick
comprehendērunt	arrested	agnōvit	recognised
Christiānus	Christian	ad salūtem	to safety
olfēcit	smelled, sniffed		

Practising the language

1 Complete each sentence with the most suitable word from the
list below, and then translate it.

ego, tū, amīcōs, leōnēs, vēndō, spectās

1 . . . . . . multās vīllās habeō.
2 ego servōs . . . . . .
3 tū gladiātōrēs . . . . . .
4 ego . . . . . . salūtō.
5 . . . . . . ancillās laudās.
6 tū . . . . . . agitās.

2 Complete each sentence with the right word, and then
translate it.

1 tū es vēnālīcius; tū servōs in forō . . . . . . (vēndō, vēndis,
vēndit)
2 ego sum gladiātor; ego in arēnā . . . . . . (pugnō, pugnās,
pugnat)
3 Fēlīx est lībertus; Fēlīx cum Caeciliō . . . . . . (cēnō, cēnās,
cēnat)

4 ego multōs spectātōrēs in amphitheātrō . . . . . . (videō, vidēs, videt)

5 tū in vīllā magnificā . . . . . . (habitō, habitās, habitat)

6 Rēgulus hodiē diem nātālem . . . . . . (celebrō, celebrās, celebrat)

7 tū saepe ad amphitheātrum . . . . . . (veniō, venīs, venit)

8 ego rem . . . . . . (intellegō, intellegis, intellegit)

About the language

1 Study the following pairs of sentences:

Pompēiānī erant īrātī.   Pompēiānī erant **īrātissimī.**
The Pompeians were angry. The Pompeians were very angry.

Milō est nōtus.   Milō est **nōtissimus.**
Milo is famous.   Milo is very famous.

Grumiō erat laetus.   Grumiō erat **laetissimus.**
Grumio was happy.   Grumio was very happy.

The words in heavy print are known as *superlatives*. Notice how they are translated in the examples above.

2 Further examples:

1 mercātor est trīstis. senex est trīstissimus.
2 canis erat ferōx. leō erat ferōcissimus.
3 amīcus fābulam longissimam nārrāvit.
4 murmillōnēs erant fortēs, sed rētiāriī erant fortissimī.

3 A few superlatives are formed in a different way:

mōns est pulcher.   mōns Vesuvius est **pulcherrimus.**
The mountain is beautiful.   Mount Vesuvius is very beautiful.

Gladiatorial shows

Among the most popular entertainments in all parts of the Roman world were shows in which gladiators fought each other. These contests were held in an amphitheatre. This was a large oval building, without a roof, in which rising tiers of seats surrounded an arena. Canvas awnings, supported by ropes and pulleys, were spread over part of the seating area to give shelter from the sun. The amphitheatre at Pompeii was large enough to contain the whole population as well as many visitors from nearby towns. Spectators paid no admission fee, as the shows were given by wealthy individuals at their own expense.

Among the many advertisements for gladiatorial shows that are to be seen painted on the walls of buildings is this one:

'Twenty pairs of gladiators, given by Lucretius Satrius Valens, priest of Nero, and ten pairs of gladiators provided by his son will fight at Pompeii from 8 to 12 April. There will also be an animal hunt. Awnings will be provided.'

Soon after dawn on the day of a show, the spectators would begin to take their places. A trumpet blared and priests came out to perform the religious ceremony with which the games began. Then the gladiators entered in procession, paraded round the arena and saluted the president of the show. The gladiators were then paired off to fight each other and the contests began.

The gladiators were usually slaves or condemned criminals; they lived and trained in a school or barracks under the supervision of a professional trainer. They were not all armed in the same way. Some, who were known as Samnites, carried an oblong shield and a short sword; others, known as Thracians, had a round shield and a sword or dagger. Another type of gladiator armed with sword and shield wore a helmet with a crest shaped like a fish; the Greek name for the fish was 'mormillos' and the gladiator was known as a 'murmillō'. The 'murmillōnēs' were often matched against the 'rētiāriī' who were armed with 'rētia' (nets) and three-pronged tridents. Other types of gladiator fought with spears, on horseback, or from chariots.

Part of the programme of one particular show, together with details of the results, reads as follows:

A Thracian versus a Murmillo
won : Pugnax from Nero's school : 3 times a winner
died : Murranus from Nero's school : 3 times a winner

A Heavily-armed Gladiator versus a Thracian
won : Cycnus from the school of Julius : 8 times a winner
set free : Atticus from the school of Julius : 14 times a winner

Chariot Fighters
won : Scylax from the school of Julius : 26 times a winner
set free : Publius Ostorius : 51 times a winner

The fight ended with the death or surrender of one of the gladiators. The illustrations below, taken from the tomb of a wealthy Pompeian, show the defeated gladiator appealing to the spectators; the victor stands by ready to kill him if they decide that he deserves to die. Notice the arm raised in appeal. The spectators indicated their wishes by turning their thumbs up or down; probably turning the thumb up towards the chest meant 'kill him', while turning it down meant 'let him live'. The final decision for death or mercy was made by the president of the games. It was not unusual for the life of the loser to be spared, especially if he were a well-known gladiator with a good number of victories to his credit. The most successful gladiators were great favourites with the crowd and received gifts of money from their admirers. One popular Pompeian gladiator was described as 'suspīrium puellārum' : 'the girls' heart-throb'. Eventually, if a gladiator survived long enough or showed great skill and courage, he would be awarded the wooden sword. This was a high honour and meant he would not have to fight again.

Many shows also offered a 'vēnātiō', a hunt of wild animals. The 'bēstiae' (wild beasts) were released from cages into the arena, where they were hunted by specially trained beast-fighters called 'bēstiāriī'. In the drawing below, you can see wolves, hares, a wild boar, a bull, a stag and a lion.

The hunters, who wore light clothing, relied upon a thrusting spear and nimble feet. By the end of the hunt all the animals and occasionally a few hunters had been killed, and their bodies were dragged out from the sandy floor of the arena to be disposed of.

**The great riot in the amphitheatre
(based on a wall-painting found in Pompeii)**

The riot at Pompeii

The story told in this Stage is based on an actual event which
occurred in A.D. 59 and is described by the Roman historian
Tacitus in these words:

'About this time, a slight incident led to a serious outburst of
rioting between the people of Pompeii and Nuceria. It occurred at a

show of gladiators, sponsored by Livineius Regulus. While hurling insults at each other, in the usual manner of country people, they suddenly began to throw stones as well. Finally, they drew swords and attacked each other. The men of Pompeii won the fight. As a result, most of the families of Nuceria lost a father or a son. Many of the wounded were taken to Rome, where the Emperor Nero requested the Senate to hold an enquiry. After the enquiry, the Senate forbade the Pompeians to hold such shows for ten years. Livineius and others who had encouraged the riot were sent into exile.'

Words and phrases checklist

agitat	chases, hunts
cōnsūmit	eats
dūcit	leads
eum	him
facile	easily
ferōx	fierce
gladius	sword
habitat	lives
hic	this
ignāvus	cowardly
incitat	urges on, encourages
nūntius	messenger
pēs	foot
porta	gate
postulat	demands
puer	boy
pugnat	fights
recumbit	lies down, reclines
saepe	often
sanguis	blood
silva	wood
spectāculum	show, spectacle
statim	at once
tōtus	whole
tuba	trumpet
vēnātiō	hunt

thermae

Quīntus ad thermās vēnit.

Quīntus servō pecūniam dedit.

amīcī Quīntum laetē salūtāvērunt,
quod diem nātālem celebrābat.

Quīntus discum novum ferēbat.
Quīntus amīcīs discum ostendit.

postquam Quīntus discum ēmīsit,
discus statuam percussit.

ēheu ! statua nāsum frāctum
habēbat.

Metella et Melissa in forō
ambulābant.
Metella fīliō dōnum quaerēbat.

fēminae mercātōrem
cōnspexērunt. mercātor
fēminīs togās ostendit.

Metella Quīntō togam ēlēgit.
Melissa mercātōrī pecūniam
dedit.

Grumiō cēnam optimam in
culīnā parābat.
coquus Quīntō cēnam parābat,
quod diem nātālem celebrābat.

multī hospitēs cum Quīntō
cēnābant.
Clēmēns hospitibus vīnum
offerēbat.

ancilla triclīnium intrāvit.
Quīntus ancillae signum dedit.
ancilla suāviter cantāvit.

thermae

cīvēs Pompēiānī trēs thermās habēbant. cīvēs cotīdiē ad thermās
ībant. servī post dominōs ambulābant. servī oleum et strigilēs
ferēbant.

   cīvēs et servī, postquam thermās intrāvērunt, āthlētās et pugilēs
vidēbant. āthlētae in palaestrā sē exercēbant. multī saliēbant, multī   5
discōs ēmittēbant. servī cīvibus discōs quaerēbant. servī,
postquam discōs invēnērunt, ad cīvēs reveniēbant. tum servī cīvibus
discōs trādēbant.

   cīvēs, postquam sē exercuērunt, apodytērium intrābant. omnēs
in apodytēriō togās dēpōnēbant, et tepidārium intrābant. cīvēs in   10
tepidāriō paulīsper sedēbant, tum ad caldārium ībant. in caldāriō
erant multae sellae. ibi dominī sedēbant et garriēbant. servī
dominīs oleum et strigilēs ferēbant. servī dominōs dīligenter
rādēbant. thermae Pompēiānōs valdē dēlectābant.

Words and phrases

thermae	baths
ībant	used to go
oleum	oil
strigilēs	strigils, scrapers
ferēbant	used to carry
āthlētās	athletes
pugilēs	boxers
in palaestrā	in the palaestra
sē exercēbant	were exercising
discōs ēmittēbant	were throwing the discus
invēnērunt	found
apodytērium	changing-room
togās	togas
tepidārium	warm room
paulīsper	for a short time
caldārium	hot room
ibi	there
garriēbant	gossiped
rādēbant	scraped

When you have read this story, answer the questions at the end.

in palaestrā

Caecilius Quīntō discum dedit, quod diem nātālem celebrābat. tum
Caecilius fīlium ad thermās dūxit, ubi palaestra erat. servus Quīntō
discum ferēbat.

Caecilius et fīlius, postquam thermās intrāvērunt, ad palaestram
contendērunt. turba ingēns in palaestrā erat. Quīntus multōs   5
iuvenēs, āthlētās, pugilēs cōnspexit. Quīntus multās statuās in
palaestrā vīdit.

'Pompēiānī āthlētīs nōtissimīs statuās posuērunt', inquit
Caecilius.

in palaestrā erat porticus ingēns. spectātōrēs in porticū stābant.   10
servī spectātōribus vīnum offerēbant.

Quīntus turbam prope porticum vīdit. āthlēta ingēns in mediā
turbā stābat.

'quis est āthlēta ille ?' rogāvit Quīntus.
'ille est Milō, āthlēta nōtissimus', respondit Caecilius.   15
Caecilius et Quīntus ad Milōnem contendērunt.

Quīntus āthlētae discum novum ostendit. Milō, postquam
discum īnspexit, ad mediam palaestram prōcessit. āthlēta
palaestram circumspectāvit et discum ēmīsit. discus longē per
aurās ēvolāvit. spectātōrēs āthlētam laudāvērunt. servus Milōnī   20
discum quaesīvit. servus, postquam discum invēnit, ad Milōnem
rediit. servus āthlētae discum offerēbat. āthlēta tamen discum nōn
accēpit.

'discus nōn est meus', inquit Milō.

servus Quīntō discum trādidit. tum iuvenis quoque discum   25
ēmīsit. discus iterum per aurās ēvolāvit. discus tamen statuam
percussit.

'ēheu !' clāmāvit Caecilius. 'statua nāsum frāctum habet.'
Quīntus rīdēbat. Pompēiānī rīdēbant. Milō tamen nōn rīdēbat.
'cūr tū nōn rīdēs ?' rogāvit iuvenis.   30
Milō erat īrātissimus.
'pestis !' respondit āthlēta. 'mea est statua !'

Words and phrases

statuās	statues	longē	far
posuērunt	have placed, have put up	per aurās ⎫ ēvolāvit ⎭	⎧ flew through ⎨ the air
porticus	colonnade	rediit	came back
offerēbant	were offering	nōn accēpit	did not accept
in mediā turbā	in the middle of the crowd	trādidit	handed over
		percussit	struck
novum	new	nāsum frāctum	a broken nose

Questions

1 Why did Caecilius give Quintus a discus ?
2 Where did Caecilius and Quintus go ?
3 What did Quintus see in the palaestra ?
4 Why were the statues in the palaestra ?
5 What happened when Milo threw the discus ?
6 What happened when Quintus threw it ?
7 What sort of person do you think Milo was ?

About the language

1 Study the following examples:

iuvenis **servō** pecūniam trādidit.
The young man handed over money to the slave.

dominus **mercātōrī** statuam ēmit.
The master bought a statue for the merchant.

Clēmēns **puellae** vīnum offerēbat.
Clemens was offering wine to the girl.

Quīntus **amīcīs** discum ostendit.
Quintus showed the discus to his friends.

servī **leōnibus** cibum dedērunt.
The slaves gave food to the lions.

The words in heavy print are in the *dative* case.

2   You have now met three cases. Notice the different ways in which they are used:

nominative **servus** dormiēbat.	The slave was sleeping.
accusative dominus **servum** excitāvit.	The master woke the slave.
dative dominus **servō** signum dedit.	The master gave a sign to the slave.

3   Compare the nominative singular with the dative singular and dative plural in each declension:

	nominative singular	*dative singular*	*dative plural*
first declension	puella	puellae	puellīs
second declension	servus	servō	servīs
third declension	mercātor	mercātōrī	mercātōribus

4   Further examples:

1 ancilla dominō cibum ostendit.
2 servus Metellae togam trādidit.
3 mercātor gladiātōribus tunicās offerēbat.
4 agricola uxōrī ānulum ēmit.

5   Notice the different cases of the words for 'I' and 'you':

nominative	*accusative*	*dative*
ego	mē	mihi
tū	tē	tibi

ego senem salūtō.	I greet the old man.
senex **mē** salūtat.	The old man greets me.
senex **mihi** statuam ostendit.	The old man shows a statue to me.
tū pictūram pingis.	You are painting a picture.
āthlēta **tē** laudat.	The athlete praises you.
āthlēta **tibi** pecūniam dat.	The athlete gives money to you.

in tabernā

Metella et Melissa ē vīllā māne discessērunt. Metella fīliō togam
quaerēbat. Metella et ancilla, postquam forum intrāvērunt,
tabernam cōnspexērunt, ubi togae optimae erant. multae fēminae
erant in tabernā. servī fēminīs stolās ostendēbant. duo gladiātōrēs
quoque in tabernā erant. servī gladiātōribus tunicās ostendēbant.   5
    mercātor in mediā tabernā stābat. mercātor erat Marcellus.
Marcellus, postquam Metellam vīdit, rogāvit,
    'quid quaeris, domina ?'
    'togam quaerō', inquit Metella. 'ego fīliō dōnum quaerō, quod
diem nātālem celebrat.'   10
    'ego multās togās habeō', respondit mercātor.
    mercātor servīs signum dedit. servī mercātōrī togās celeriter
trādidērunt. Marcellus fēminīs togās ostendit. Metella et ancilla
togās īnspexērunt.
    'hercle !' clāmāvit Melissa. 'hae togae sunt sordidae.'   15
    Marcellus servōs vituperābat.
    'sunt intus togae splendidae', inquit Marcellus.
    Marcellus fēminās intus dūxit. mercātor fēminīs aliās togās
ostendit. Metella Quīntō mox togam splendidam ēlēgit.
    'haec toga, quantī est ?' rogāvit Metella.   20
    'quīnquāgintā dēnāriōs cupiō', respondit Marcellus.
    'quīnquāgintā dēnāriōs cupis ! furcifer !' clāmāvit Melissa. 'ego
tibi decem dēnāriōs offerō.'

Words and phrases

māne	in the morning	ēlēgit	chose
domina	madam	haec	this
dōnum	present, gift	quantī est ?	how much is it ?
hae togae	these togas	quīnquāgintā dēnāriōs	fifty denarii
sordidae	dirty	cupiō	I want
intus	inside	decem	ten
aliās	other		

'quadrāgintā dēnāriōs cupiō', respondit mercātor.

'tibi quīndecim dēnāriōs offerō', inquit ancilla.   25

'quid ? haec est toga pulcherrima ! quadrāgintā dēnāriōs
cupiō', respondit Marcellus.

'tū nimium postulās', inquit Metella. 'ego tibi trīgintā dēnāriōs
dō.'

'cōnsentiō', respondit Marcellus.   30

Melissa Marcellō pecūniam dedit. Marcellus Metellae togam
trādidit.

'ego tibi grātiās maximās agō, domina', inquit Marcellus.

Words and phrases

quadrāgintā	forty	trīgintā	thirty
quīndecim	fifteen	cōnsentiō	I agree
nimium	too much	ego grātiās agō	I thank

Practising the language

1   Complete each sentence with a word that makes good sense,
    and then translate it.

for example: mercātōrēs fēminīs tunicās . . . . . . (audīvērunt,
              ostendērunt, timuērunt)
              mercātōrēs fēminīs tunicās ostendērunt.
              The merchants showed the tunics to the women.

1 ancilla dominō vīnum . . . . . . (timuit, dedit, salūtāvit)
2 iuvenis puellae stolam . . . . . . (ēmit, vēnit, prōcessit)
3 fēminae servīs tunicās . . . . . . (intrāvērunt, quaesīvērunt,
  contendērunt)
4 cīvēs āctōrī pecūniam . . . . . . (laudāvērunt, vocāvērunt,
  trādidērunt)
5 centuriō mercātōribus decem dēnāriōs . . . . . . (trādidit, ēmit,
  vīdit)

2 Complete each sentence with the right word, and then translate it.

for example: gladiātōrēs amīcīs togās . . . . . . (ostendit, ostendērunt)
gladiātōrēs amīcīs togās ostendērunt.
The gladiators showed the togas to their friends.

1 puella gladiātōribus tunicās . . . . . . (dedit, dedērunt)
2 cīvēs Milōnī statuam . . . . . (posuit, posuērunt)
3 mercātor amīcō vīnum . . . . . (trādidit, trādidērunt)
4 coquus ancillae ānulum . . . . . (ēmit, ēmērunt)
5 vēnālīciī fēminīs servōs . . . . . (ostendit, ostendērunt)
6 servus Quīntō discum . . . . . (quaesīvit, quaesīvērunt)
7 nautae uxōribus stolās pulchrās . . . . . ēlēgit, ēlēgērunt)
8 Clēmēns et Grumiō Metellae cēnam optimam . . . . . .
(parāvit, parāvērunt)

3 This exercise is based on the story 'in tabernā', on page 9. Read the story again. Complete each of the sentences below with the right word or phrase, and then translate it.

1 Metella . . . . . ad forum ambulāvit. (cum Quīntō, cum Grumiōne, cum Melissā)
2 postquam forum intrāvērunt, ... cōnspexērunt. (portum, tabernam, vīllam)
3 Metella gladiātōrēs et . . . . . . in tabernā vīdit. (āctōrēs, fēminās, centuriōnēs)
4 servī fēminīs . . . . . . ostendēbant. (tunicās, stolās, togās)
5 servī gladiātōribus . . . . . . ostendēbant. (togās, stolās, tunicās)
6 mercātor servīs . . . . . dedit. (signum, togam, gladium)
7 servī mercātōrī . . . . . . trādidērunt. (togam, togās, stolās)
8 mercātor . . . . . vituperāvit, quod togae erant sordidae. (gladiātōrēs, fēminās, servōs)

in apodytēriō

duo servī in apodytēriō stant. servī sunt Sceledrus et Anthrāx.

Sceledrus: cūr nōn labōrās, Anthrāx? num dormīs?
Anthrāx: quid dīcis? dīligenter labōrō. ego cīvibus togās custōdiō.
Sceledrus: togās custōdīs? mendāx es!
Anthrāx: cūr mē vituperās? mendāx nōn sum. togās custōdiō.   5
Sceledrus: tē vituperō, quod fūr est in apodytēriō, sed tū nihil facis.
Anthrāx: ubi est fūr? fūrem nōn videō.
Sceledrus: ecce! homō ille est fūr. fūrem facile agnōscō.
            (Sceledrus Anthrācī fūrem ostendit. fūr togam suam dēpōnit et
            togam splendidam induit. servī ad fūrem statim currunt.)   10
Anthrāx: quid facis? furcifer! haec toga nōn est tua!
fūr: mendāx es! mea est toga! abī!
Sceledrus: tē agnōscō! pauper es, sed togam splendidam geris.
            (mercātor intrat. togam frūstrā quaerit.)
mercātor: ēheu! ubi est toga mea? toga ēvānuit!   15
            (mercātor circumspectat.)
            ecce! hic fūr togam meam gerit!
fūr: parce! parce! pauperrimus sum . . . uxor mea est
            aegra . . . decem līberōs habeō . . .

mercātor et servī fūrem nōn audiunt, sed eum ad iūdicem trahunt.   20

Words and phrases

induit	is putting on
abī !	go away !
pauper	a poor man
geris	you are wearing
parce !	mercy !
aegra	sick, ill
līberōs	children

The baths

About the middle of the afternoon, Caecilius would make his way, with a group of friends, to the public baths. These were not a swimming-pool but something rather like a modern Turkish bath. Let us imagine that Caecilius decides to visit the baths situated just to the north of the forum, and let us follow him through the various rooms and activities.

At one of the entrances, he pays a small admission fee to the 'ostiārius' (doorkeeper) and then goes to the 'palaestra' (exercise area). This is an open space surrounded by a colonnade, rather like a large peristylium. Here he spends a little time greeting other friends and taking part in some of the popular exercises, which included throwing a large ball from one to another, wrestling, and fencing with wooden swords. These games were not taken too seriously but were a pleasant preparation for the bath which followed.

From the palaestra, Caecilius and his friends walk along a passage into a large hall known as the 'apodytērium', or changing-room. Here they remove all their clothes and hand them to one of the slave attendants, who places them in niches arranged in rows along the wall. Leaving the apodyterium, they pass through an arched doorway into the 'tepidārium' (warm room) and there spend a little time sitting on benches round the wall in a warm steamy atmosphere, perspiring gently and getting their bodies ready for the higher temperatures in the next room. This is the 'caldārium', or hot room. At one end of the caldarium there was a large marble bath, oblong in shape, and stretching across the full width of the room. This bath was filled with hot water in which the bathers sat or wallowed. The Romans did not have soap, but used olive oil instead. After soaking in the bath, Caecilius summons a slave to rub him down with the oil that he has brought with him in a little pot. For this rubbing down, Caecilius lies on a marble slab while the slave works the oil into his skin, and then gently removes it and the impurities with a blunt metal scraper known as a strigil.

MEN'S BATHS
1 apodytērium
2 tepidārium
3 caldārium
4 frigidārium
5 furnace

WOMEN'S BATHS
A apodytērium
B tepidārium
C caldārium

S shop

Plan of Forum Baths

Next comes the masseur to massage skin and muscles. Refreshed by this treatment, Caecilius then goes to the large stone tub at the other end of the caldarium for a rinse down with cold water.

Before dressing again he might well visit the 'frigidārium' (cold room) and there take a plunge in a deep circular pool of unheated water, followed by a brisk rub down with his towel.

The Roman taking his bath did not hurry, nor did he take it quietly. He liked the company of his friends and he was not shy about expressing his enjoyment. Here is a description of the sounds that could be heard, written by Seneca, who lived in Rome uncomfortably close to a set of baths.

'I am surrounded by uproar. My lodgings are over a set of baths. Just imagine the babel of sounds that strike my ears. When the athletic gentlemen below are exercising themselves, lifting lead weights, I can hear their grunts. I can hear the whistling of their breath as it escapes from their lungs. I can hear somebody enjoying a cheap rub down and the smack of the masseur's hands on his shoulders. If his hand comes down flat, it makes one sound; if it comes down hollowed, it makes another. Add to this the noise of a brawler or pickpocket being arrested down below, the racket made by the man who likes to sing in his bath or the sound of enthusiasts who hurl themselves into the water with a tremendous splash. Next, I can hear the screech of the hair-plucker, who advertises himself by shouting. He is never quiet except when he is plucking hair and making his victim shout instead. Finally, just imagine the cries of the cake-seller, the sausage-man, and the other food-sellers as they advertise their goods round the bath, all adding to the din.'

Clearly this was more than just a place to get clean in. It was much more like a popular social club.

The Romans were not the first people to build public baths. This was one of the many things they learned from the Greeks. But with their engineering skill the Romans greatly improved the methods of heating them. The previous method had been to heat the water in tanks over a furnace and to stand braziers in the warm room and the hot room to keep up the air temperature. The braziers were not very efficient and they failed to heat the floor.

In the first century B.C., a Roman invented the first central heating system. The furnace was placed below the floor level; the floor was supported on small brick piles leaving space through which hot air from the furnace could circulate. In this way, the floor was warmed from below. The hot bath was placed near the furnace and a steady temperature was maintained by the hot air passing immediately below. Later, flues were placed in the walls and warm air from beneath the floor was drawn up through them. This ingenious heating system was known as a hypocaust. It was used not only in baths but also in private houses, particularly in the colder parts of the Roman empire. Many examples have been found in Britain. Charcoal was the fuel most commonly burnt in the furnaces.

Plan of hypocaust

Words and phrases checklist

agnōscit	recognises	īnspicit	looks at,
celebrat	celebrates		examines
celeriter	quickly	iterum	again
cīvis	citizen	manet	remains, stays
cupit	wants	medius	middle
dat	gives	mox	soon
diēs	day	nōtus	well known,
diēs nātālis	birthday		famous
ēmittit	throws,	offert	offers
	sends out	ostendit	shows
exercet	exercises	paulīsper	for a short time
fert	brings, carries	post	after
homō	man	revenit	comes back,
hospes	guest		returns
ille	that	suus	his
		trādit	hands over

rhētor

Rōmānus dīcit,
   'nōs Rōmānī sumus architectī. nōs viās et pontēs aedificāmus.'

'nōs Rōmānī sumus agricolae. nōs fundōs optimōs habēmus.'

Graecus dīcit,
 'nōs Graecī sumus sculptōrēs. nōs statuās pulchrās facimus.'

'nōs Graecī sumus pictōrēs. nōs pictūrās pingimus.'

Rōmānus dīcit,
  'vōs Graecī estis ignāvī. vōs āctōrēs semper spectātis.'

Graecus dīcit,
  'vōs Rōmānī estis barbarī. vōs semper pugnātis.'

Rōmānus dīcit,
  'nōs sumus callidī. nōs rēs ūtilēs facimus.'

Graecus dīcit,
  'nōs sumus callidiōrēs quam vōs. nōs Graecī Rōmānōs docēmus.'

contrōversia

Quīntus amīcum Graecum habēbat. amīcus erat Alexander. Quīntus et Alexander ad palaestram ībant, ubi rhētor Graecus erat. hic rhētor erat Theodōrus et prope palaestram habitābat. in palaestrā erat porticus longa, ubi Theodōrus iuvenēs docēbat. postquam ad hanc porticum vēnērunt, Alexander et Quīntus   5
rhētōrem audīvērunt. rhētor iuvenibus contrōversiam nūntiāvit, 'Graecī sunt meliōrēs quam Rōmānī.'

Quīntus vehementer exclāmāvit,
'minimē ! nōs Rōmānī sumus meliōrēs quam Graecī.'
Theodōrus, postquam hanc sententiam audīvit, respondit,   10
'haec est tua sententia. nōs tamen nōn sententiam quaerimus, nōs argūmentum quaerimus.' tum Quīntus rhētōrī et amīcīs argūmentum explicāvit.

'nōs Rōmānī sumus fortissimī. nōs barbarōs ferōcissimōs superāmus. nōs imperium maximum habēmus. nōs pācem   15
servāmus. vōs Graecī semper contentiōnēs habētis. vōs semper estis turbulentī.

'nōs sumus architectī optimī. nōs viās et pontēs ubīque aedificāmus. urbs Rōma est maior quam omnēs urbēs.

'postrēmō nōs Rōmānī dīligenter labōrāmus. deī igitur nōbīs   20
imperium maximum dant. vōs Graecī estis ignāvī. vōs numquam labōrātis. deī vōbīs nihil dant.'

postquam Quīntus hanc sententiam explicāvit, iuvenēs Pompēiānī vehementer plausērunt et eum laudāvērunt. deinde Alexander surrēxit. iuvenēs Pompēiānī tacuērunt et Alexandrum intentē   25
spectāvērunt.

'vōs Rōmānī estis miserandī. vōs imperium maximum habētis, sed vōs estis imitātōrēs; nōs Graecī sumus auctōrēs. vōs Graecās statuās spectātis, vōs Graecōs librōs legitis, Graecōs rhētōrēs audītis. vōs Rōmānī estis rīdiculī, quod estis Graeciōrēs quam nōs   30
Graecī !'

iuvenēs, postquam Alexander sententiam suam explicāvit, rīsērunt. tum Theodōrus nūntiāvit,
'Alexander victor est. argūmentum optimum explicāvit.'

Words and phrases

contrōversia	debate	maior quam	greater than,
rhētor	teacher		bigger than
docēbat	used to teach	postrēmō	lastly
meliōrēs quam	better than	deī	gods
minimē !	no !	dant	give
sententiam	opinion	deinde	then
argūmentum	proof	surrēxit	got up
barbarōs	barbarians	miserandī	pathetic, pitiful
imperium	empire	imitātōrēs	imitators
pācem	peace	auctōrēs	creators
architectī	builders, architects	librōs	books
pontēs	bridges	legitis	read
ubīque	everywhere	rīsērunt	laughed
aedificāmus	build		

statuae

postquam Theodōrus Alexandrum laudāvit, iuvenēs Pompēiānī ē
porticū discessērunt. Alexander et Quīntus ad vīllam ambulābant,
ubi Alexander et duo frātrēs habitābant.

Alexander frātribus dōnum quaerēbat, quod diem nātālem
celebrābant.   5

in viā īnstitor parvās statuās vēndēbat et clāmābat:
'statuae ! optimae statuae !'

Alexander frātribus statuās ēmit. statuae erant senex, iuvenis,
puella pulchra. Alexander, postquam statuās ēmit, ad vīllam cum
Quīntō contendit.   10

duo frātrēs in hortō sedēbant. Diodōrus pictūram pingēbat,
Thrasymachus librum Graecum legēbat. postquam Alexander et
Quīntus vīllam intrāvērunt, puerī ad eōs cucurrērunt. Diodōrus
statuās cōnspexit.

frātrēs	brothers	ad eōs	to them
īnstitor	pedlar		

'Alexander, quid portās?' inquit.   15

'vōs estis fēlīcēs', inquit Alexander. 'ego vōbīs dōnum habeō
quod vōs diem nātālem celebrātis. ecce !' Alexander frātribus
statuās ostendit.

'quam pulchra est puella', inquit Diodōrus. 'dā mihi puellam !'
'minimē ! frāter, dā mihi puellam !' clāmāvit Thrasymachus.   20
puerī dissentiēbant et lacrimābant.

'hercle ! vōs estis stultissimī puerī !' clāmāvit Alexander īrātus.
'semper dissentītis, semper lacrimātis. abīte ! abīte ! ego statuās
retineō !'

puerī, postquam Alexander hoc dīxit, abiērunt. Diodōrus   25
pictūram in terram dēiēcit, quod īrātus erat. Thrasymachus librum
in piscīnam dēiēcit, quod īrātissimus erat.

tum Quīntus dīxit,

'Alexander, dā mihi statuās ! Thrasymache ! Diodōre ! venīte
hūc ! Thrasymache, ecce ! ego tibi senem dō, quod senex erat   30
philosophus. Diodōre, tibi iuvenem dō, quod iuvenis erat pictor.
ego mihi puellam dō, quod ego sum sōlus ! vōsne estis contentī ?'

'sumus contentī', respondērunt puerī.

'ecce, Alexander', inquit Quīntus, 'vōs Graeculī estis optimī
artificēs sed turbulentī. nōs Rōmānī vōbīs pācem damus.'   35

'et vōs praemium accipitis', susurrāvit Thrasymachus.

Words and phrases

fēlīcēs	lucky	venīte hūc !	come here !
quam !	how !	philosophus	philosopher
dā !	give !	sōlus	lonely
dissentiēbant	were arguing	vōsne estis	are you satisfied ?
stultissimī	very stupid	contentī ?	
retineō	am keeping	Graeculī	poor Greeks
abiērunt	went away	artificēs	artists
in terram	onto the ground	praemium	profit
dēiēcit	threw	susurrāvit	whispered,
in piscīnam	into the fish-pond		muttered

About the language

1 In this Stage, you have met sentences with 'we' and 'you':

nōs labōrāmus.   vōs labōrātis.
We work.   You work.

nōs currimus.   vōs curritis.
We run.   You run.

Notice that 'vōs labōrātis' and 'vōs curritis' are *plural* forms. They are used when 'you' refers to more than one person.

2 You have now met the whole of the present tense:

(ego)	portō	I carry
(tū)	portās	you (singular) carry
	portat	he carries
(nōs)	portāmus	we carry
(vōs)	portātis	you (plural) carry
	portant	they carry

3 Notice that 'nōs' and 'vōs' are not strictly necessary, since the endings '-mus' and '-tis' make it clear that 'we' and 'you' are being spoken about. The Romans normally left out 'nōs' and 'vōs', just as they left out 'ego' and 'tū'.

4 Further examples:
1 nōs pugnāmus. vōs dormītis.
2 vōs clāmātis. nōs audīmus.
3 ambulāmus. dīcimus. vidēmus.
4 vidētis. nūntiātis. intrāmus.

5 The Latin for 'we are' and 'you (plural) are' is as follows:

nōs sumus iuvenēs.   vōs estis pictōrēs.
We are young men.   You are artists.

nōs sumus fortēs.   vōs estis ignāvī.
We are brave.   You are cowardly.

So the complete present tense of 'sum' is:

(ego)	sum	I am
(tū)	es	you (singular) are
	est	he is
(nōs)	sumus	we are
(vōs)	estis	you (plural) are
	sunt	they are

When you have read this story, answer the questions at the end.

ānulus Aegyptius

Syphāx in tabernā sedēbat. caupō Syphācī vīnum dedit. Syphāx
caupōnī ānulum trādidit.

'pecūniam nōn habeō', inquit, 'quod Neptūnus nāvem meam
dēlēvit.'

caupō, postquam ānulum accēpit, eum īnspexit.   5

'ānulus antīquus est', inquit.

'ita vērō, antīquus est', Syphāx caupōnī respondit. 'servus
Aegyptius mihi ānulum dedit. servus in pȳramide ānulum
invēnit.'

caupō, postquam tabernam clausit, ad vīllam suam festīnāvit. 10
caupō uxōrī ānulum ostendit. caupō uxōrī ānulum dedit, quod
ānulus eam dēlectāvit.

uxor postrīdiē ad urbem contendēbat. subitō servus ingēns in viā
appāruit. pecūniam postulāvit. fēmina, quod erat perterrita, servō
pecūniam dedit. servus ānulum cōnspexit. ānulum postulāvit. 15
fēmina servō eum trādidit.

fēmina ad tabernam rediit et marītum quaesīvit. mox eum invēnit. caupō incendium spectābat. ēheu ! taberna ardēbat ! fēmina marītō rem tōtam nārrāvit.

'ānulus īnfēlīx est', inquit caupō. 'ānulus tabernam meam   20
dēlēvit.'

servus ingēns, postquam pecūniam et ānulum cēpit, ad urbem contendit. subitō trēs servōs cōnspexit. servī inimīcī erant. inimīcī, postquam pecūniam cōnspexērunt, servum verberābant. servus fūgit, sed ānulum āmīsit.   25

Grumiō cum Poppaeā ambulābat. ānulum in viā invēnit.
'quid vidēs ?' rogāvit Poppaea.
'ānulum videō', inquit. 'ānulus Aegyptius est.'
'euge !' inquit Poppaea. 'ānulus fēlīx est.'

Words and phrases

Aegyptius	Egyptian	eam	her
caupō	innkeeper	postrīdiē	on the next day
Neptūnus	Neptune	marītum	husband
	(god of the sea)	incendium	blaze, fire
dēlēvit	has destroyed	ardēbat	was on fire
antīquus	old, ancient	īnfēlīx	unlucky
in pȳramide	in a pyramid	āmīsit	lost
clausit	shut		

Questions

1 How did Syphax pay for his drink ?
2 Why did he pay for it in this way ?
3 How did the innkeeper comment on what Syphax had given him ?
4 Where, according to Syphax, had it come from ?
5 What did the innkeeper do with the gift ?
6 What happened to the innkeeper's wife ?
7 What happened to the innkeeper ?
8 What happened to the big slave in the city ?
9 What did Grumio see in the road and what did Poppaea think of it ?
10 Who have the ring at the end of the story ? What do you expect to happen as a result ?

Practising the language

1 Complete each sentence with the most suitable phrase from the list below, and then translate it.

fābulam agimus, contrōversiam habēmus, cibum offerimus, stolās compōnimus, pānem parāmus

1 nōs sumus rhētōrēs Graecī; nōs in palaestrā . . . .
2 nōs sumus āctōrēs nōtissimī; nōs in theātrō . . . .
3 nōs sumus ancillae pulchrae; nōs fēminīs . . . .
4 nōs sumus coquī; nōs dominīs . . . .
5 nōs sumus pistōrēs; nōs cīvibus . . . .

2 Complete each sentence with the most suitable word from the list below and then translate it.

servī, āthlētae, pictōrēs, vēnālīciī, gladiātōrēs

1 vōs estis. . . . . . callidī; vōs pictūrās magnificās pingitis.
2 vōs estis . . . . . . fortēs; vōs in arēnā pugnātis.
3 nōs sumus . . . . . . ; nōs in thermīs togās custōdīmus.
4 vōs servōs in forō vēnditis, quod vōs estis . . . .
5 nōs ad palaestram contendimus, quod nōs sumus . . . .

About the language

1 Study the following pairs of sentences:

nōs Rōmānī sumus callidī.   We Romans are clever.
nōs Rōmānī sumus **callidiōrēs** We Romans are cleverer
quam vōs Graecī.   than you Greeks.

nōs Rōmānī sumus fortēs.   We Romans are brave.
nōs Rōmānī sumus **fortiōrēs** We Romans are braver than
quam vōs Graecī.   you Greeks.

The words in heavy print are known as *comparatives*. They are used to compare two things or groups with each other. In the examples above, the Romans are comparing themselves with the Greeks.

2 Further examples:

1 Pompēiānī sunt stultī. Nūcerīnī sunt stultiōrēs quam Pompēiānī.

2 Diodōrus erat īrātus, sed Thrasymachus erat īrātior quam Diodōrus.

3 mea vīlla est pulchra, sed tua vīlla est pulchrior quam mea.

3 The following word forms its comparative in an unusual way:

Nūceria est magna.   Nuceria is large.

Rōma est **maior** quam Nūceria. Rome is larger than Nuceria.

Schools

Quintus would have first gone to school when he was about seven years old. Like other Roman schools, the one that Quintus attended would have been small and consisted of about thirty pupils and a teacher known as the 'ludī magister'.

Parents were not obliged by law to send their children to school, and those who wanted education for their children had to pay for it. The charges were not high and the advantages of being able to read and write were so widely appreciated that many people were prepared to pay for their sons to go to school at least for a few years. Daughters were usually educated at home, but rich people sometimes sent them to the schoolmaster.

On the journey between home and school, pupils were normally escorted by a slave known as a 'paedagōgus'. Another slave carried their books and writing materials.

The materials that Quintus used for writing were rather different from ours. Frequently he wrote on 'tabulae' (wooden tablets) coated with a thin film of wax; and he inscribed the letters on the wax surface with a thin stick of metal, bone or ivory. This stick was called a 'stilus'. The end opposite the writing point was flat so that it could be used to rub out mistakes and make the wax smooth again. Several tablets were strung together to make a little writing-book. At other times he wrote with ink on papyrus, a material that looked rather like modern paper but was rougher in texture. It was manufactured from the fibres of the papyrus reed that grew along the banks of the River Nile in Egypt. For writing on papyrus he used either a reed or a goose-quill sharpened and split at one end like the modern pen-nib. Ink was made from soot and resin or other gummy substances, forming a paste that was thinned by adding water. The best inks were so hard and durable that they are perfectly legible even today on the pieces of papyrus that have survived.

In the drawing below you see tabulae joined together, stili, inkwells and a goose-quill, and rolls of papyrus.

**Writing
materials**

Pictures of scenes in school show that there were generally no desks and no blackboard. Pupils sat on benches or stools, resting tablets on their knees. The master sat on a high chair overlooking his class. Discipline was usually strict and sometimes harsh.

The school-day began early and lasted for six hours with a short break at midday. Holidays were given on public festivals and on every ninth day which was a market-day; during the hot summer months fewer pupils attended lessons, and some schoolmasters may have closed their schools altogether from July to October.

When he was eleven, Quintus would have moved to a secondary school run by a 'grammaticus'. This teacher introduced his pupils to the work of famous Greek and Roman writers, beginning with the *Iliad* and *Odyssey* of Homer. Then the pupils moved on to the tragedies of Aeschylus, Sophocles and Euripides, Greek playwrights who had written their plays in Athens in the fifth century B.C. The Roman poet most frequently read at school was Virgil. Besides listening to works of literature and reading them aloud, the pupils learnt long passages by heart; many educated people could remember these passages in later life and quote or recite them. The pupils were also taught a little history and geography, mainly in order to understand references to famous people and places mentioned in the literature.

When he left the grammaticus at the age of fifteen or sixteen, Quintus would have a good knowledge of Greek as well as Latin. This knowledge of Greek not only introduced the pupils to a culture which the Romans greatly admired and which had inspired much of their own civilisation, but it was also very useful because Greek was widely spoken in the countries of the eastern Mediterranean where Roman merchants and government officials frequently travelled on business.

Many children finished their schooling at eleven years of age, having learnt to read, write and do simple arithmetic. Most of those who went on to the school of the grammaticus finished at about fifteen; but a few then proceeded to a third stage. They went to a 'rhētor', like Theodorus in our story. This teacher, who was often a highly educated Greek, gave more advanced lessons in literature and trained his students in the art of public speaking. This was a very important skill for young men who expected to take part in public life. They needed it to present cases in the law courts, to express their opinions in council meetings, to address the people at election time and in many other situations. The rhetor taught the rules for making different kinds of speeches and made his students practise arguing for and against a point of view. Students also learned how to vary their tone of voice and emphasise their words with gestures.

We have not so far mentioned the teaching of science and technical subjects in Roman schools. It is true that the Greeks had made important discoveries in mathematics, philosophy and some aspects of physics; it is also true that the Romans were experienced in such things as the methods of surveying and the use of concrete in building. But these things played little part in school work. The purpose of ordinary Roman schools was to teach those things which were thought to be most necessary for civilised living: the ability to read and write, a knowledge of simple arithmetic, the appreciation of fine literature and the ability to speak and argue convincingly. Philosophy and science were taught in only a few special schools; and technical skills were learned by becoming an apprentice in a trade or business.

Words and phrases checklist

abit	goes away	nōs	we
accipit	accepts	nūntiat	announces
callidus	clever, cunning	pāx	peace
capit	takes	portus	harbour
contentus	satisfied	quam	than
exclāmat	exclaims	semper	always
frāter	brother	sententia	opinion
hercle !	by Hercules !	servat	saves, looks after
imperium	empire	sōlus	alone
inimīcus	enemy	tacet	is silent, is quiet
invenit	finds	uxor	wife
it	goes	vehementer	violently, loudly
liber	book	vōs	you (plural)

PISTORES
RUFUM
II VIRUM ROGANT

candidātī

cīvēs in forō candidātōs spectant.

agricolae clāmant,
    'nōs candidātum optimum habēmus.'
    'candidātus noster est Lūcius.'
    'nōs Lūciō favēmus.'

mercātōrēs agricolīs respondent,
    'nōs candidātum optimum habēmus.'
    'candidātus noster est mercātor.'
    'nōs mercātōrī favēmus.'

pistōrēs in forō clāmant,
  'nōs pistōrēs candidātum optimum habēmus.'
  'candidātus noster est pistor.'
  'nōs pistōrī crēdimus.'

iuvenēs pistōribus respondent,
  'nōs iuvenēs candidātum optimum habēmus.'
  'candidātus noster est āthlēta.'
  'nōs āthlētae crēdimus.'

fūrēs clāmant,
  'nōs quoque candidātum habēmus.'
  'candidātus noster est fūr.'
  'nōs candidātō nostrō nōn crēdimus
  sed favēmus.'

Marcus et Quārtus

Marcus Tullius et Quārtus Tullius erant frātrēs. Marcus et
Quārtus in vīllā contentiōnem habēbant. Marcus Quārtō dīxit,
  'Āfer candidātus optimus est. Āfer multās vīllās et multās
tabernās habet. Pompēiānī Āfrō favent, quod vir dīves est.'
  'minimē! Holcōnius candidātus optimus est', Quārtus frātrī   5
respondit. 'Holcōnius est vir nōbilis. Pompēiānī Holcōniō crēdunt,
quod pater senātor erat.'
  Quārtus, quod erat īrātissimus, ē vīllā discessit. Quārtus sibi
dīxit,
  'frāter meus est stultissimus. gēns nostra Holcōniō semper favet.'   10
  Quārtus per viam ambulābat et rem cōgitābat. subitō parvam
tabernam cōnspexit, ubi scrīptor habitābat. scrīptor Sulla erat.
Quārtus, postquam tabernam vīdit, cōnsilium cēpit. tabernam
intrāvit et Sullam ad vīllam suam invītāvit.

  postquam ad vīllam vēnērunt, Quārtus Sullae mūrum ostendit.   15
'scrībe hunc titulum!' inquit. 'scrībe "Quārtus et frāter Holcōniō
favent. Quārtus et frāter Holcōniō crēdunt ".'
  Quārtus scrīptōrī decem dēnāriōs dedit.
  'placetne tibi?' rogāvit Quārtus.
  'mihi placet', Sulla Quārtō respondit. Sulla, postquam dēnāriōs   20
accēpit, titulum in mūrō scrīpsit.

Words and phrases

candidātus	candidate	scrīptor	sign-writer
favent	favour, give support to	cōnsilium cēpit	had an idea
dīves	rich	mūrum	wall
vir nōbilis	a man of noble birth	scrībe!	write!
crēdunt	trust, have faith in	titulum	notice, slogan
sibi dīxit	said to himself	placetne tibi?	does it suit you?
gēns nostra	our family	scrīpsit	wrote
rem cōgitābat	was considering the problem		

Sulla

Marcus ē vīllā vēnit. Sullam vīdit. titulum cōnspexit. postquam
titulum lēgit, īrātus erat. Marcus scrīptōrem valdē vituperābat.
    'frāter tuus mē ad vīllam invītāvit', inquit Sulla. 'frāter tuus mihi
decem dēnāriōs dedit.'
    'frāter meus est stultior quam asinus', Marcus Sullae respondit. 5
'in vīllā nostrā ego sum dominus, quod sum senior. Sulla, ērāde
illam īnscrīptiōnem ! scrībe titulum novum !'
    Marcus Sullae quīndecim dēnāriōs dedit.
    'placetne tibi ?' rogāvit.
    'mihi placet', Sulla Marcō respondit. Sulla, postquam 10
īnscrīptiōnem ērāsit, hunc titulum scrīpsit, 'Marcus et frāter Āfrō
favent. Marcus et frāter Āfrō crēdunt.'
    Marcus erat laetissimus et frātrem ē vīllā vocāvit. Marcus frātrī
titulum novum ostendit. Quārtus, postquam titulum lēgit, īrātus
erat. Quārtus Marcum pulsāvit. tum frātrēs in viā pugnābant ! 15
    'Marce ! Quārte ! dēsistite ! intrō īte !' clāmāvit Sulla. 'cōnsilium
optimum habeō.'
    postquam frātrēs vīllam intrāvērunt, Sulla celeriter rem cōnfēcit.
    duōs titulōs in mūrō scrīpsit. tum frātrēs ē vīllā vocāvit.
    scrīptor frātribus mūrum ostendit. ecce ! Marcus hunc titulum 20
vīdit: 'Marcus Āfrō favet. Āfer est candidātus optimus.'
    'euge ! hic titulus mē valdē dēlectat', inquit Marcus.
    Quārtus alterum titulum in mūrō cōnspexit:
'Quārtus Holcōniō favet. Holcōnius est candidātus optimus.'
    Quārtus quoque laetissimus erat. 25
    frātrēs Sullae trīgintā dēnāriōs dedērunt. Sulla rīdēbat.
    postquam Marcus et Quārtus discessērunt, tertium titulum addidit:
    'Marcus et Quārtus sunt līberālissimī.'

asinus	ass, donkey	intrō īte !	go inside !
senior	the elder	rem cōnfēcit	finished the job
ērāde !	rub out ! erase !	tertium	third
īnscrīptiōnem	writing	addidit	added
ērāsit	rubbed out, erased	līberālissimī	very generous
dēsistite !	stop !		

Lūcius Spurius Pompōniānus

in vīllā

Grumiō ē culīnā contendit. Clēmēns Grumiōnem videt.

Clēmēns: babae! togam splendidam geris!
Grumiō: placetne tibi?
Clēmēns: mihi placet. quō festīnās, Grumiō?
Grumiō: ad amphitheātrum contendō. Āfer fautōrēs exspectat.   5
Clēmēns: num tū Āfrō favēs? Caecilius Holcōniō favet.
Grumiō: Āfer fautōribus quīnque dēnāriōs prōmīsit. Holcōnius fautōribus duōs dēnāriōs tantum prōmīsit. ego Āfrō faveō, quod vir līberālis est.
Clēmēns: sed tū servus es. cīvis Pompēiānus nōn es. Āfer cīvibus   10
Pompēiānīs pecūniam prōmīsit.
Grumiō: Clēmēns, hodiē nōn sum Grumiō. hodiē sum Lūcius Spurius Pompōniānus!
Clēmēns: Lūcius Spurius Pompōniānus! mendācissimus coquus es!   15
Grumiō: minimē! hodiē sum pistor Pompēiānus. hodiē nōs pistōrēs ad amphitheātrum convenīmus. nōs Āfrum ad forum dūcimus, ubi cīvēs ōrātiōnēs exspectant. ego ad amphitheātrum contendō. tū mēcum venīs?
Clēmēns: tēcum veniō. Āfrō nōn faveō. dēnāriōs nōn cupiō, sed dē   20
tē sollicitus sum. rem perīculōsam suscipis.
(exeunt.)

Words and phrases

babae !	hey !	convenīmus	gather, meet
quō ?	where ?	ōrātiōnēs	speeches
fautōrēs	supporters	mēcum	with me
quīnque	five	dē tē	about you
prōmīsit	promised	perīculōsam	dangerous
tantum	only	suscipis	you are taking on
mendācissimus	very deceitful	exeunt	they go out

prope amphitheātrum

multī pistōrēs ad amphitheātrum conveniunt. Grumiō et Clēmēns ad hanc turbam festīnant.

dīvīsor:	festīnāte! festīnāte! nōs Āfrum exspectāmus.
Grumiō:	salvē, dīvīsor! ego sum Lūcius Spurius Pompōniānus et hic *(Grumiō Clēmentem pulsat)* servus meus est. ego et 5 Āfer amīcissimī sumus.
dīvīsor:	ecce quīnque dēnāriī! *(dīvīsor Grumiōnī dēnāriōs dat. dīvīsor Grumiōnī fūstem quoque trādit.)*
Grumiō:	Āfer mihi dēnāriōs, nōn fūstem prōmīsit. 10
Clēmēns:	Āfer vir līberālis est.
Grumiō:	tacē, pessime serve!
dīvīsor:	fūstēs ūtilissimī sunt. Holcōnius et amīcī sunt in forō.
pistor:	ecce Āfer! Āfer adest! *(Āfer et fautōrēs per viās ad forum contendunt.)* 15

Words and phrases

dīvīsor	distributor (hired to distribute bribes at elections)
festīnāte !	hurry !
amīcissimī	very friendly, very good friends
tacē !	shut up ! be quiet !
ūtilissimī	very useful

in forō

pistōrēs cum Clēmente et cum Grumiōne Āfrum ad forum dūcunt.

pistor prīmus:	Pompēiānī Āfrō favent.
pistor secundus:	Āfer est melior quam Holcōnius.
pistor tertius:	nōs Āfrō crēdimus.
Clēmēns:	Grumiō! in forō sunt Holcōnius et amīcī. 5 Holcōnium et amīcōs videō.

Grumiō:	euge! fēminās videō, ancillās videō, puellās . . .
	ēheu! Caecilium videō! Caecilius cum Holcō-
	niō stat! ad vīllam reveniō!
Clēmēns:	Grumiō, manē! 10
	(Grumiō fugit.)
mercātor prīmus:	Holcōnius est vir nōbilis.
mercātor secundus:	Holcōnius melior est quam Āfer.
mercātor tertius:	nōs mercātōrēs Holcōniō favēmus.
	(pistōrēs et mercātōrēs conveniunt. īrātī sunt.) 15
pistor prīmus:	Holcōnius est asinus. vōs quoque estis asinī,
	quod Holcōniō crēditis.
mercātor prīmus:	Āfer est caudex. vōs quoque estis caudicēs,
	quod Āfrō crēditis.
pistor secundus:	amīcī! mercātōrēs nōs 'caudicēs' vocant. nōs 20
	nōn sumus caudicēs. fortissimī sumus. fūstēs
	habēmus.
mercātor secundus:	amīcī! pistōrēs nōs 'asinōs' vocant. nōs nōn
	sumus asinī. nōs fortiōrēs sumus quam pis-
	tōrēs. magnōs fūstēs habēmus. 25
	(mercātōrēs et pistōrēs in forō pugnant.)

    caudex   blockhead, idiot

in culīnā

Clēmēns in culīnā sedet. Grumiō intrat.

Clēmēns: salvē, Pompōniāne! hercle! toga tua scissa est!

Grumiō: ēheu! Holcōnius et amīcī in forō mē cēpērunt. postquam
fūstem meum cōnspexērunt, clāmābant, 'ecce pistor
fortis!' tum mercātōrēs mē verberāvērunt. dēnāriōs   5
meōs rapuērunt. nunc nūllōs dēnāriōs habeō.

Clēmēns: ego decem dēnāriōs habeō!

Grumiō: decem dēnāriōs?

Clēmēns: Caecilius mihi decem dēnāriōs dedit, quod servus fidēlis
sum. postquam pistōrēs et mercātōrēs pugnam commīs-   10
ērunt, Caecilius mē cōnspexit. duo pistōrēs Caecilium
verberābant. dominus noster auxilium postulābat.

Caecilius mēcum ē forō effūgit. dominus noster mihi
decem dēnāriōs dedit, quod līberālis est.
Grumiō: Caecilius est . . .   15
Clēmēns: valē, Pompōniāne!
Grumiō: quō festīnās, Clēmēns?
Clēmēns: ad portum festīnō. ibi Poppaea mē exspectat. placetne
tibi?
Grumiō: mihi nōn placet!   20

Words and phrases

scissa   torn   auxilium   help
rapuērunt   seized, grabbed   effūgit   escaped

About the language

1   In Stage 9, you met the dative case:

Quīntus **servō** pecūniam dedit.   Quintus gave money **to
                                        the slave.**

2   In Stage 11, you have met some further examples:

mercātōrēs **agricolīs**   The merchants reply **to the
respondent.   farmers.**
Quārtus **Holcōniō**   Quartus gives support **to
favet.   Holconius.**
nōs **pistōrī** crēdimus.   We have faith **in the baker.**

3   Some of the sentences above can be translated more simply:

Quārtus Holcōniō favet.   Quartus supports Holconius.
nōs pistōrī crēdimus.   We trust the baker.

4   Further examples:

1 nōs Āfrō favēmus.
2 vōs Holcōniō crēditis.
3 mercātōrēs candidātō nostrō nōn crēdunt.
4 pistōrēs mercātōribus respondent.

5   Notice the dative of 'nōs' and 'vōs':

nōs sumus fortēs. deī **nōbīs** imperium dant.
We are brave. The gods give an empire to us.

vōs estis ignāvī. deī **vōbīs** nihil dant.
You are cowardly. The gods give nothing to you.

6   Notice the following use of the dative:

'placetne **tibi**?'   '**mihi** placet.'
'Is it pleasing to you ?' 'It is pleasing to me.'

There are many other ways of translating these examples,
such as:

'Does it please you ?' 'It pleases me.'
'Is it all right for you ?' 'Yes, it is.'

Practising the language

1   Complete each sentence with the right word from the list below,
and then translate it. Do not use any word more than once.

contendō	faveō
contendis	favēs
contendimus	favēmus
contenditis	favētis

1 ego ad forum . . . . . . ego sum fautor.
2 tū Āfrō . . . . tū es caudex.
3 ego Holcōniō . . . . . ., quod Holcōnius est candidātus
  optimus.
4 nōs Holcōniō nōn . . . . . ., quod Holcōnius est asinus.
5 Clēmēns, cūr tū ad portum . . . . .?
6 vōs Āfrō . . . . . ., quod vōs estis pistōrēs.
7 nōs ad vīllam . . . . . ., quod in forō sunt Holcōnius et amīcī.
8 ēheu ! cūr ē forō . . . . . .? vōs dēnāriōs meōs habētis !

2 Complete each sentence with the right word, and then translate it.

1 Quārtus Sullae decem dēnāriōs dedit. Sulla . . . . . in mūrō scrīpsit. (titulus, titulum)
2 fūr vīllam intrābat. subitō . . . . . . lātrāvit. (canis, canem)
3 multī candidātī sunt in forō. ego . . . . . . videō. (Holcōnius, Holcōnium)
4 ego ad portum currō. . . . . . . mē exspectat. (ancilla, ancillae)
5 hodiē ad urbem contendō. in amphitheātrō sunt . . . . . (gladiātor, gladiātōrēs)
6 rhētor est īrātus. rhētor . . . . . . exspectat. (puerī, puerōs)
7 fēminae sunt in tabernā. mercātōrēs fēminīs . . . . . . ostendunt. (stolae, stolās)
8 postquam Holcōnius et amīcī Grumiōnem cēpērunt, quīnque . . . . . rapuērunt. (dēnāriī, dēnāriōs)

About the language

1 So far you have met the following ways of asking questions in Latin:

1 (From Stage 4 onwards) By means of a question-word such as 'quis ?' 'quid ?' 'ubi ?' 'cūr ?'

quis est Quīntus ?	Who is Quintus ?
quid tū facis ?	What are you doing ?
ubi est ānulus ?	Where is the ring ?
cūr lacrimās ?	Why are you crying ?

2 (From Stage 4 onwards) By tone of voice, indicated in writing by means of a question-mark:

tū pecūniam dēbēs ?	Do you owe the money ?
tū ānulum habēs ?	Do you have the ring ?

3 (From Stage 10 onwards) By adding '-ne' to the first word of the sentence:

vōsne estis contentī ?	Are you satisfied ?
placetne tibi ?	Does it please you ?

4 (From Stage 7 onwards)   By means of the question-word
'num ?' This word is used to suggest that the answer to the
question will be 'no'. Notice the different ways of translating
it:

num tū timēs ?	Surely you're not afraid ?
	You're not afraid, are you ?
num vīnum bibis ?	Surely you're not drinking wine ?
	You're not drinking wine, are you ?

2   Further examples:

1 cūr tū in hortō labōrās ?
2 quis est āthlēta ille ?
3 tū discum habēs ?
4 vōsne estis īrātī ?
5 ubi sunt mercātōrēs ?
6 quid quaeris, domina ?
7 tūne Pompēiānus es ?
8 quis vīnum portat ?
9 cēnam parās ?
10 num cēnam parās ?

Local government and elections

Pompeii, like other Roman towns, was responsible for managing its
own local government. Every year two pairs of officials were elected
by the people. The senior pair, called 'duovirī', were responsible for
hearing evidence and giving judgement in the law court. The other
pair, called 'aedilēs', had the task of supervising the public markets,
the police force, the baths, places of public entertainment, the water
supply and sewers. It was their duty to see that the public services
were efficiently run and the local taxes spent wisely.

In addition to these four officials, there was a town council of one hundred leading citizens, most of whom had already served as duoviri or aediles. New members were chosen not by the people but by the council itself.

The Pompeians took local politics seriously and the annual elections, which were held at the end of March, were very lively. As soon as the names of candidates were published, election fever gripped the town. Slogans appeared on the walls, groups of 'fautōrēs' (supporters) held processions through the streets and the candidates spoke at public meetings in the forum.

Many of the thousands of wall notices found in Pompeii refer to the elections held there in March A.D. 79. Here are two of them:

'Casellius for aedile.'

'We want Titus Claudius Verus for duovir.'

It appears that these notices were often painted on the walls at night by torchlight, either because the streets were then more or less deserted and so there was less risk of trouble from rival supporters, or because it was easier at night to put up a ladder for an hour or two without causing congestion on the pavements.

Political supporters represented all kinds of people and interests. Sometimes they were groups of neighbours, 'vīcīnī', who lived in the same area as the candidate. They would certainly include the candidate's personal friends and his clientes. Often, however, a candidate was nominated and supported by a particular trade group. One notice reads:

'The barbers recommend Trebius for aedile.'

Another says:

'Innkeepers, vote for Sallustius Capito !'

Mule-drivers, pack-carriers, bakers, fishermen : all expressed their support for their chosen candidate.

This method of electioneering by wall slogans naturally invited replies by rival supporters. One candidate, Vatia, was made to look ridiculous by this comment:

'All the people who are fast asleep vote for Vatia.'

Pompeian women did not have the right to vote. Only adult male citizens were allowed to cast votes in the voting hall on election day. Nevertheless, women certainly took a lively interest in local politics and supported the various candidates vigorously.They painted slogans and marched through the streets carrying placards.

The candidates themselves wore a specially whitened toga in order to be easily recognised. The word 'candidātus' is connected with 'candidus' which means 'dazzling white'. As they walked around greeting voters, they were accompanied by agents, who praised their qualities, made promises on their behalf, and distributed bribes in the form of money. This financial bribery was illegal but was widely practised. Legal forms of persuasion included promises of games and entertainments if the candidate won. In fact, it was expected that those who were elected would show their gratitude to the voters by putting on splendid shows in the theatre and amphitheatre at their own expense.

A successful candidate would also be expected to contribute from his own wealth to the construction or repair of public buildings. We know that the temple of Fortuna Augusta, situated just to the north of the forum, was built largely by the generosity of Marcus Tullius who owned the whole of the site on which it was built. The family of the Holconii, whose names often appear in the lists of Pompeian duoviri and aediles, were connected with the building of the large theatre, and another wealthy family, the Flacci, helped to pay for other civic buildings. The Flacci also had a reputation for putting on first class entertainments.

This tradition of public service was encouraged by the emperors and was an important part of Roman public life. It made it possible for a small town like Pompeii to enjoy benefits which could not have been paid for by local taxes alone. It also meant that men who wanted to take part in the government of their town had to be wealthy. The number of families in Pompeii who could afford to hold office regularly was about fifty.

Although public service was unpaid and was not a means of making money, it gave a man a position of importance in his town. The wide seats in the front row of the theatre, which gave a close-up view of the chorus and actors, were reserved for him; he also had a special place close to the arena in the amphitheatre. In due course the town council might erect a statue to him and he would have his name inscribed on any building to whose construction or repair he had contributed. The Romans were not particularly modest people.

They were eager for honour and fame amongst their fellow citizens. There was therefore no shortage of candidates to compete for these rewards at election time.

Caecilius, who in many ways was an outstanding citizen and who had made a considerable fortune by his ability as a businessman, was prevented by law from standing as a candidate for public office because he was the son of a freedman. His son Quintus, however, could have been a candidate if had wished, when he was old enough.

We said at the beginning of this account of local government that Pompeii was free to run its own affairs. But if the local officials were unable to preserve law and order, the central government at Rome might take over and run the town. This actually happened after the famous riot in A.D. 59 described in Stage 8, when the people of nearby Nuceria quarrelled with the Pompeians at a gladiatorial show given by Livineius Regulus, and many were killed or wounded. The Nucerians complained to the Emperor Nero; Regulus himself was sent into exile and games in Pompeii were banned for ten years. In the following year, A.D. 60, Nero dismissed the duoviri and appointed a special officer or 'praefectus' to run the affairs of the town. This was a strong sign of official disapproval and two years passed before the local people were again trusted to look after themselves.

Words and phrases checklist

convenit	gathers, meets	prīmus	first
crēdit	trusts, believes	prōmittit	promises
dē	about	pugna	fight
favet	supports	rapit	seizes
gēns	family	secundus	second
invītat	invites	senātor	senator
legit	reads	sollicitus	worried, anxious
līberālis	generous	stultus	stupid
minimē !	no !	tertius	third
mūrus	wall	ūtilis	useful
noster	our	valē !	goodbye !
nunc	now	verberat	strikes, beats
placet	it pleases	vir	man

mōns Vesuvius

Syphāx et Celer in portū stābant.
amīcī montem spectābant.

Syphāx amīcō dīxit,
'ego prope portum servōs
vēndēbam. ego subitō
sonōs audīvī.'

Celer Syphācī respondit,
'tū sonōs audīvistī. ego tremōrēs
sēnsī. ego prope montem
ambulābam.'

Poppaea et Lucriō in ātriō
stābant. sollicitī erant.

Poppaea Lucriōnī dīxit,
'ego in forō eram. ego tibi
togam quaerēbam. ego
nūbem mīrābilem cōnspexī.'

Lucriō Poppaeae respondit,
'tū nūbem cōnspexistī. ego
cinerem sēnsī. ego flammās
vīdī.'

Marcus et Quārtus in forō erant.
Sulla ad frātrēs contendit.

Sulla frātribus dīxit,
'ego ad theātrum contendēbam.
ego sonōs audīvī et tremōrēs
sēnsī. vōs sonōs audīvistis ?
vōs tremōrēs sēnsistis ?'

frātrēs Sullae respondērunt,
'nōs tremōrēs sēnsimus
et sonōs audīvimus.
nōs nūbem mīrābilem vīdimus.
nōs sollicitī sumus.'

When you have read this story, answer the questions at the end.

tremōrēs

Caecilius cum Iūliō cēnābat. Iūlius in vīllā splendidā prope
Nūceriam habitābat.

Iūlius Caeciliō dīxit, 'ego sollicitus sum. ego in hortō heri
ambulābam et librum legēbam. subitō terra valdē tremuit. ego
tremōrēs sēnsī. quid tū agēbās ?'   5
'ego servō epistulās dictābam', inquit Caecilius. 'ego quoque
tremōrēs sēnsī. postquam terra tremuit, Grumiō tablīnum intrāvit
et mē ad hortum dūxit. nōs nūbem mīrābilem vīdimus.'
'vōs timēbātis ?' rogāvit Iūlius.
'nōs nōn timēbāmus', Caecilius Iūliō respondit. 'ego, postquam 10
nūbem cōnspexī, familiam meam ad larārium vocāvī. tum nōs
laribus sacrificium fēcimus.'
'vōs fortissimī erātis', clāmāvit Iūlius. 'vōs tremōrēs sēnsistis, vōs
nūbem cōnspexistis. vōs tamen nōn erātis perterritī.'
'nōs nōn timēbāmus, quod nōs laribus crēdēbāmus', inquit 15
Caecilius. 'iamprīdem terra tremuit. iamprīdem tremōrēs vīllās et
mūrōs dēlēvērunt. sed larēs vīllam meam et familiam meam
servāvērunt. ego igitur sollicitus nōn sum.'
subitō servus triclīnium intrāvit.
'domine, Clēmēns est in ātriō. Clēmēns ex urbe vēnit. Caecilium 20
quaerit', servus Iūliō dīxit.
'nōn intellegō', Caecilius exclāmāvit. 'ego Clēmentem ad fundum
meum māne mīsī.'
servus Clēmentem in triclīnium dūxit.
'cūr tū ē fundō discessistī ? cūr tū ad hanc vīllam vēnistī ?' 25
rogāvit Caecilius.
Clēmēns dominō et Iūliō rem tōtam nārrāvit.

Words and phrases

tremōrēs	tremors	familiam	household
tremuit	shook	larārium	domestic shrine
sēnsī	felt	laribus	household gods
agēbās	were doing	sacrificium	sacrifice
epistulās	letters	iamprīdem	a long time ago
dictābam	was dictating	fundum	farm
nūbem	cloud		

Questions

1 Why was Iulius worried ?
2 What had Caecilius been doing when the tremors began ?
3 What did Caecilius and Grumio see when they went into the garden ?
4 What did Caecilius do then ?
5 Why was Caecilius so sure that his household gods would look after him ?
6 What news did Iulius' slave bring ?
7 Why did this news puzzle Caecilius ?

ad urbem

'ego ad fundum tuum contendī', Clēmēns dominō dīxit. 'ego vīlicō
epistulam tuam trādidī. postquam vīlicus epistulam lēgit, nōs
fundum et servōs īnspiciēbāmus. subitō nōs ingentēs sonōs
audīvimus. nōs tremōrēs quoque sēnsimus. tum ego montem
spectāvī et nūbem mīrābilem vīdī.'   5
  'quid vōs fēcistis ?' rogāvit Iūlius.
  'nōs urbem petīvimus, quod valdē timēbāmus', respondit
Clēmēns. 'ego, postquam urbem intrāvī, clāmōrem ingentem audīvī. multī Pompēiānī per viās currēbant. fēminae cum īnfantibus per
urbem festīnābant. fīliī et fīliae parentēs quaerēbant. ego ad vīllam   10
nostram pervēnī, ubi Metella et Quīntus manēbant. Quīntus mē ad
tē mīsit, quod nōs omnēs perterritī erāmus.'
  Caecilius ad urbem contendit, quod sollicitus erat. Iūlius et
Clēmēns quoque ad urbem festīnāvērunt. maxima turba viās
complēbat, quod Pompēiānī ē vīllīs festīnābant.   15
  prope urbem Holcōnium cōnspexērunt. Holcōnius cum servīs ad
portum fugiēbat.
  'cūr vōs ad urbem contenditis ? cūr nōn ad portum fugitis ?'
rogāvit Holcōnius.
  'ad vīllam meam contendō', Caecilius Holcōniō respondit.   20
'Metellam et Quīntum quaerō. tū Metellam vīdistī ? Quīntum
cōnspexistī ?'
  'ēheu !' clāmāvit Holcōnius. 'ego vīllam splendidam habēbam. in
vīllā erant statuae pulchrae et pictūrae pretiōsae. iste mōns vīllam
meam dēlēvit; omnēs statuae sunt frāctae.'   25
  'sed, amīce, tū uxōrem meam vīdistī ?' rogāvit Caecilius.
  'ego nihil dē Metellā sciō. nihil cūrō', respondit Holcōnius.
  'furcifer !' clāmāvit Caecilius. 'tū vīllam tuam āmīsistī. ego
uxōrem meam āmīsī !'
  Caecilius, postquam Holcōnium vituperāvit, ad urbem   30
contendit.

Words and phrases

vīlicō	bailiff, manager
sonōs	noises
fīliae	daughters
parentēs	parents
pervēnī	reached, arrived at
iste mōns	that mountain
scio	know
nihil cūrō	I don't care

The eruption of Mount Vesuvius in March 1944

ad vīllam

in urbe pavor maximus erat. cinis iam dēnsior incidēbat. flammae
ubīque erant. Caecilius et amīcī, postquam urbem intrāvērunt,
vīllam petēbant. sed iter erat difficile, quod multī Pompēiānī viās
complēbant. Caecilius tamen per viās fortiter contendēbat.

nūbēs iam dēnsissima erat. subitō Iūlius exclāmāvit,   5
'vōs ad vīllam contendite ! ego nōn valeō.'
statim ad terram dēcidit exanimātus. Clēmēns Iūlium ad
templum proximum portāvit.

'tū optimē fēcistī', Caecilius servō dīxit. 'tū Iūlium servāvistī. ego
tibi lībertātem prōmittō.'   1

tum Caecilius ē templō discessit et ad vīllam cucurrit.
Clēmēns cum Iūliō in templō manēbat. tandem Iūlius respīrāvit.
'ubi sumus ?' rogāvit.
'sumus tūtī', servus Iūliō respondit. 'dea Īsis nōs servāvit.
postquam tū in terram dēcidistī, ego tē ad hoc templum portāvī.'   1
'tibi grātiās maximās agō, quod tū mē servāvistī', inquit Iūlius.
'sed ubi est Caecilius ?'
'dominus meus ad vīllam contendit', respondit Clēmēns.
'ēheu ! stultissimus est Caecilius !' clāmāvit Iūlius. 'sine dubiō
Metella et Quīntus mortuī sunt. ego ex urbe quam celerrimē
discēdō. tū mēcum venīs ?'

'minimē, amīce !' Clēmēns Iūliō respondit. 'ego dominum meum
quaerō !'

Words and phrases

pavor	panic	exanimātus	unconscious
cinis	ash	templum	temple
iam	now	proximum	nearest
dēnsior	thicker	lībertātem	freedom
incidēbat	was falling	respīrāvit	recovered breath,
flammae	flames		recovered consciousness
iter	journey, progress	tūtī	safe
difficile	difficult	dea	goddess
valeō	I feel well	sine dubiō	without doubt

fīnis

iam nūbēs ātra ad terram dēscendēbat; iam cinis dēnsissimus
incidēbat. plūrimī Pompēiānī iam dē urbe suā dēspērābant. multī
in flammīs perībant. Clēmēns tamen nōn dēspērābat, sed obstinātē
vīllam petīvit, quod Caecilium quaerēbat. tandem ad vīllam pervēn⤻
it. sollicitus ruīnās spectāvit. tōta vīlla ardēbat. Clēmēns fūmum   5
ubīque vīdit. per ruīnās tamen fortiter contendit et dominum suum
vocāvit. Caecilius tamen nōn respondit. subitō canis lātrāvit. servus
tablīnum intrāvit, ubi canis erat. Cerberus dominum custōdiēbat.

Caecilius in tablīnō moribundus iacēbat. mūrus sēmirutus eum
paene cēlābat. Clēmēns dominō vīnum dedit. Caecilius, postquam   10
vīnum bibit, sēnsim respīrāvit.

'quid accidit, domine ?' rogāvit Clēmēns.

'ego ad vīllam vēnī', inquit Caecilius. 'Metellam nōn vīdī !
Quīntum nōn vīdī ! vīlla erat dēserta. tum ego ad tablīnum
contendēbam. subitō terra tremuit et pariēs in mē incidit. tū   15
es servus fidēlis. abī ! ego tē iubeō. dē vītā meā dēspērō. Metella et
Quīntus periērunt. nunc ego quoque sum moritūrus.'

Clēmēns recūsāvit. in tablīnō obstinātē manēbat. Caecilius
iterum clāmāvit:

'Clēmēns, abī ! tē iubeō. fortasse Quīntus superfuit. quaere   20
Quīntum ! hunc ānulum Quīntō dā !'

Caecilius, postquam Clēmentī ānulum suum trādidit, statim
exspīrāvit. Clēmēns dominō trīste valedīxit et ē vīllā discessit.
Cerberus tamen in vīllā mānsit. dominum frūstrā custōdiēbat.

Words and phrases

fīnis	end
ātra	black
dēscendēbat	was coming down
plūrimī	most
perībant	were dying, were perishing
obstinātē	stubbornly
ruīnās	ruins, wreckage
fūmum	smoke
moribundus	almost dead
sēmirutus	half-collapsed
sēnsim	slowly, gradually
accidit	happened
pariēs	wall
iubeō	order
moritūrus	going to die
recūsāvit	refused
superfuit	has survived
exspīrāvit	died
trīste	sadly
valedīxit	said goodbye

About the language

1 In Stage 6 you met the imperfect and perfect tenses:

imperfect	*perfect*
portābat	portāvit
he was carrying	he carried
portābant	portāvērunt
they were carrying	they carried

2 In Stage 12 you have met the imperfect and perfect tenses in sentences with 'I', 'you' and 'we':

imperfect	*perfect*
(ego) portābam	(ego) portāvī
I was carrying	I carried
(tū) portābās	(tū) portāvistī
you (singular) were carrying	you (singular) carried
(nōs) portābāmus	(nōs) portāvimus
we were carrying	we carried
(vōs) portābātis	(vōs) portāvistis
you (plural) were carrying	you (plural) carried

'ego', 'tū', 'nōs' and ' vōs' are usually left out.

3 The words for 'was' and 'were' are as follows:

(ego)	eram	I was
(tū)	erās	you (singular) were
	erat	he was
(nōs)	erāmus	we were
(vōs)	erātis	you (plural) were
	erant	they were

The destruction and excavation of Pompeii

On the night of 23-4 August A.D. 79, it rained hard; a strong wind blew and earth tremors were felt. During the following morning, Vesuvius, which had been an inactive volcano for many centuries, erupted with enormous violence. A huge mass of mud poured down the mountainside and swallowed the town of Herculaneum; hot stones and ash descended in vast quantities on Pompeii, burying everything to a depth of four-and-a-half to six metres (fifteen to twenty feet). Most people, with vivid memories of the earthquake seventeen years before, fled into the open countryside carrying a few possessions, but others remained behind, hoping that the storm would pass. They died, buried in the ruins of their homes or suffocated by sulphur fumes.

The eruption of Mount Vesuvius in A.D. 79

The next day, the whole area was a desert of white ash. Here and there the tops of buildings could be seen, and little groups of survivors struggled back to salvage what they could. They dug tunnels to get down to their homes and rescue furniture, valuables and paintings. But nothing could be done to excavate and rebuild the town itself. The site was abandoned; thousands of refugees made new homes in Naples and other Campanian towns. Gradually the ruins collapsed, a new layer of soil covered the site and Pompeii disappeared from view.

During the Middle Ages, nobody knew exactly where the town lay. Only a vague memory survived in the name 'cività' by which the local people still called the low hill. But what city it was or whether there really was a city buried there, they did not know and certainly did not care.

The first remains were found in 1594 when an Italian architect called Fontana was constructing a water channel from the River Sarno to a nearby town. He discovered the remains of buildings and an inscription. But these were misunderstood as it was thought that a villa belonging to the famous Roman politician, Pompeius, had been discovered. Nothing much was done for another 150 years, until in 1748, Charles III, King of Naples, began to excavate the site in search of treasure. In 1763, the treasure seekers realised they were exploring the lost city of Pompeii. At Herculaneum the excavations were much more difficult because the volcanic mud had turned to hard rock and the town lay up to twelve metres (forty feet) below the new ground level. Tunnelling down was slow and dangerous work.

In the early days of excavation, no effort was made to uncover the sites in an orderly way; the methods of modern archaeology were unknown. The excavators were not interested in uncovering towns in order to learn about the people who had lived there, but were looking for jewellery, pictures, bronze statues and other works of art, which were then taken away to decorate the palaces of kings and rich men.

At the beginning of the nineteenth century, however, the looting was stopped and systematic excavation began. Section by section, the soil and rubble were cleared. The most fragile and precious objects were taken to the National Museum in Naples, but everything else was kept where it was found. As buildings were uncovered, they were partly reconstructed with original materials to preserve them and make them safe for visitors.

From time to time, archaeologists still find a hollow space in the ash where an object of wood or other organic material has perished. To find out what it was, they pour liquid plaster into the hole, and when it has hardened they carefully remove the surrounding ash, and are left with a perfect image of the original object. In this way, many wooden doors and shutters have been discovered, and also bodies of human beings and animals.

The work is not yet finished. Only about three-fifths of Pompeii has so far been uncovered and less of Herculaneum. Whenever a new house is opened up, the archaeologist finds it just as it was abandoned. He may discover the remains of a meal, pots on the stove, coins in the tablinum, lampstands in various rooms, paintings (often only slightly damaged) on the walls, the lead pipes which supplied water to the fountains in the garden, brooches, needles, jars of cosmetics, shoes and writing-tablets; in fact all the hundreds of small things that went to make up a Roman home. If he is lucky, he may also discover the name of the family that lived there.

Thus, through the efforts of the archaeologist, a remarkably detailed picture of the life of this ordinary Roman town has emerged from the disaster which destroyed it 2,000 years ago.

Words and phrases checklist

āmittit	loses
cinis	ash
complet	fills
custōdit	guards
dēnsus	thick
epistula	letter
flamma	flame
fortiter	bravely
frūstrā	in vain
fugit	runs away, flees
fundus	farm
iacet	lies
iam	now
igitur	therefore
incidit	falls
mīrābilis	strange, wonderful
mittit	sends
mōns	mountain
nūbēs	cloud
optimē	very well
paene	nearly, almost
sentit	feels
tandem	at last
templum	temple
terra	ground, land
timet	is afraid, fears

You have also met the following numbers:

ūnus	one
duo	two
trēs	three